Advance Praise for *Stop Falling for the Okeydoke*

You hit the nail right on the head!
Bishop Felton Edwin May (Retired) of the United Methodist Church

****

This book is a very personal and powerful examination of the "lie of race" that has served those in power well throughout our history and right up to the present day. This overt yet invisible political sleight of hand has been used to divide us and subvert the ability of the vast majority of us as citizens to work together to achieve our common interests. Rev. Tillett's warm and accessible approach dispels pervasive myths and untruths and illuminates the history, science and politics of this destructive "lie." His book is a rousing call to wake up and stop falling for the "okeydoke." As my father Howard Zinn said: "…when we organize with one another, when we get involved, when we stand up and speak out together, we can create a power no government can suppress."

Myla Kabat-Zinn (daughter of Dr. Howard Zinn, author of A People's History of the United States)

****

I have known Stephen Tillett for many years, and he has been making big moves all his life. He has been a change-agent in college, serving as pastor to diverse congregations, as a military chaplain and as a community leader where he serves as an NAACP branch president. And now he is leading the way again with this incredible book! Read it, then share it with friends and family! You will see why Stephen continues to lead, even on the challenging topic of race! This book is leading edge thinking and it will have a big impact on America and the world!"

Dr. Willie Jolley, Best selling author of A Setback Is A Setup For A Comeback and Achieving Greatness with An Attitude of Excellence

Stop Falling for the
OKEYDOKE

How the Lie of "Race" Continues to Undermine Our Country

STEPHEN A. TILLETT

STOP FALLING FOR THE OKEYDOKE
HOW THE LIE OF "RACE" CONTINUES TO
UNDERMINE OUR COUNTRY

iUniverse books may be ordered through booksellers or by contacting:

iUniverse
1663 Liberty Drive
Bloomington, IN 47403
www.iuniverse.com
1-800-Authors (1-800-288-4677)

ISBN: 978-1-5320-2229-6 (sc)
ISBN: 978-1-5320-2231-9 (hc)
ISBN: 978-1-5320-2230-2 (e)

Library of Congress Control Number: 2017907309

Print information available on the last page.

iUniverse rev. date: 05/22/2017

To my children, Drew, Lena, and Sophia. Our "children are the living messages we send to a time we will not see." (Postman, 1984) I have the hope that the world in which you—and your children, after you—live will become a more decent and familial place where people truly "will not be judged by the color of their skin, but by the content of their character."

I offer special thanks to Lena for the birthday gift of Howard Zinn's *A People's History of the United States.* It served as inspiration for this project and introduced me to history I never knew!

Thanks to my "Momma Bear," Bernice Johnson Tillett, for using your nonpareil proofreading skills as a "retired" English teacher to help me bring this project to fruition.

I also dedicate this book to the memory of my father, Malcolm Tillett, for sharing his love of history with me. I love it to this day. Thanks, too, for all the debates on the issues of the day. I miss you and hope to make you proud.

Last, but certainly not least, I thank my sweetie, Sherita, for her support, encouragement, suggestions, and, most of all, patience with me as I took over / converted a spare bedroom into *another* office dedicated to making this long-held dream a reality. Thank you for giving me a peaceful place to be creative and complete this project that has meant so much to me. I love you to life!

ACKNOWLEDGEMENTS

Wali Uqdah, Jr, photography, and for inspiration with the cover concept.

Martin Gesis, model, and for "getting" the cover concept and bringing it to life.

Duane, Kevin and the Alphagraphics team for the cover art.

Thanks to family, friends and colleagues who took the time to read drafts of this book and offer constructive observations and encouragement. Thank you Akeda, Alice, Barbara, Derek, Felton, Michele, Natalie and Sherita.

Myla Kabat-Zinn for your generosity of spirit and encouragement.

Dr. Willie Jolley for your support and wise counsel.

Dr. Unnia Pettus of Pettus PR, LLC for your nonpareil public relations support.

Dawn Jones and 29Eleven Media for your graphics skills and website design, etc…

Many thanks to the editors, production and promotions staff at iUniverse for helping to bring this publication to fruition and presenting it to the world!

FOREWORD

I am and will forever be grateful for you thinking enough of me to read your manuscript. Needless to say, "Timeless"! The artistry of woven truths orchestrating melodies of words burst within the innermost bowels of my soul. At times my spirit shouted, "Write My Brother - You Better Write," "You Better Preach," and "Speak The Word!"

Your thoughtfulness and intentionality was very present throughout, which I appreciated. The inclusion of specific historical facts and statistical data secured fidelity. The inclusion of graphs also provided greater depth and clarity. When I reached the last two pages and started reading a song I had never read or heard; it truly summed up the very essence of your book. Last but not least, every ethnicity should be able to relate because at the end of the day, we are all one race.

As MLK stated so eloquently and you reiterated to be truth...

"Our aim must never be to defeat or humiliate the White man, but to win his friendship and understanding. We must come to see that the end we **seek is a society at peace with itself, a society that can live with its conscience.** *And that will be a day not of the white man, not of the black man. That will be the day of man as man."*

I would highly recommend STOP FALLING FOR THE OKEYDOKE to readers of all genres and ages. Although some may differ as it relates to all ages but if a child can read this book, he/she would challenge their vocabulary, fluency, comprehension and dispel "untruths" in many of their textbooks.

KEEP WRITING!

Dr. Akeda Pearson-Stenbar
Professor at Bowie State University
President and CEO, Premier Training and Professional Development
Services

PREFACE

I have been very fortunate to live a life that has exposed me to any number of different experiences. Beginning with the privilege of growing up in a country that was shedding its *dejure* segregation, I was exposed, both in the neighborhood where I grew up, and the schools that I attended, to a more diverse expression of humanity. My career as a pastor and a military chaplain, combined with experiences as a chaplain to a football team and having played sports in high school and college has given me a more comprehensive exposure to the fundamental essence of who people are and how and why they are the way they are. Had my exposure to "others" been limited to what I saw on television and in media, I would have had a fundamental misunderstanding about human nature in diverse ethnic groups.

I consider myself a political scientist and an observer of people. While I am no scientist, in the context of genetics, I have used critical thinking, read a lot and spent many hours speaking with and interacting with people different from my family of origin. I have concluded that when all the labels and categories are taken away, we are fundamentally the same. We are all human beings trying to find our way. We are at least aware of the *"Golden Rule"* if we don't yet live by it. "Do unto others as you would have them do unto you." Our personal family environments and community and national history have made it more difficult to observe that rule, in part due to the lie of "race" that has been taught to every man, woman, boy and girl since birth. This book is my modest effort to go against the tide of convention and share the many reasons why we need to Stop Falling for the Okeydoke!

CONTENTS

INTRODUCTION

Recently, I was privileged to have lunch with one of my respected elders, a man who has spent the better part of six decades in ministry. Some of that time, he was on the front lines of the civil rights movement in the states where he served. Now, as an octogenarian, as he is looking back over his life at the struggles, challenges, and the victories he felt that our community had won, he is contemplative. He was also juxtaposing those feelings with his frustrations with where we seem to be now as a nation, and he is vastly disappointed with what he is seeing. Battles, like voting rights, that had been fought and won before are being relitigated now. It feels very much like "déjà vu all over again," he declared.

We have just suffered through one of the most nonsensical presidential elections in American history. There are increasing instances of racial animus all around us. Some of the challenges facing our community are things we thought had been dealt with years ago, but now, as with an unwelcome, faded rerun, what can I say but "here we go again." Candidates were willing to say almost anything to sway angry, frustrated voters. The level of demagoguery in this election harkens back to much darker periods in our nation's history (Strom Thurmond c. 1948, George Wallace c. 1968). The Bible has been prescient in speaking to this regrettable dynamic: "What has been will be again, what has been done will be done again; there is nothing new under the sun" (Ecclesiastes 1:9). Alas, we continue to repeat our mistakes and make vigorous assertions about things that are demonstrably untrue. As a nation, we are not yielding to "the better angels of our nature" but instead seem to follow after things that have a visceral appeal but no moral or righteous outcome. Again, scripture speaks to this phenomenon: "For the time will come when people will not put up with sound doctrine. Instead, to suit their own desires, they will gather around them a great number of 'teachers' [quotation marks added] to say what their itching ears want to hear. They will turn their ears away from the truth and turn aside to myths" (2 Timothy 4:3–4).

In this era when electronic information (and misinformation and disinformation) is at our very fingertips, rather than doing the hard work of objective, personal research and examining the lessons of history—things that have actually happened—people instead seem content to seek after and receive only those things that confirm their previously held beliefs. Worse than that, whereas new generations had before exceeded the limitations of their parents and grandparents, there seems to be a fair number of young people in this era who are being forced to live in a world dominated by those shopworn assumptions and prejudices of their foreparents. If we are to truly go forward and progress as a nation and a planet, the young people must lead the way!

I have had it in my mind and heart to write this book for the past several years. The more time passes, the more exigent it appears that I must take the time to sit down and write all that has been percolating in my mind and in my soul. I do not begin this project as if writing on a blank slate. There is a great deal of writing that has been done on topics related to what we call race—human ethnicity—from the vantage points of history, sociology, and science. In this book, I will quote from some of them and seek to provide a reference for every quote I am using to state my case that it is *past* time for a new paradigm in matters of interethnic relations and how this impacts every area of our lives including our economic statuses and our politics. These are areas that have benefitted the most by our being Balkanized [definition: to divide into smaller, mutually hostile groups]. I do not intend to reinvent the wheel but will instead quote generously from historians, scientists, and others as I make my case. I will sometimes parenthetically interject my own thoughts and observations, in the midst of the writings of others to "foot stomp" (as we say in the military) points that warrant extra attention. Once this has been published, you will have all the references that will enable you to investigate for yourselves and try to learn the lessons that history is trying to teach us, free from the "political correctness" (whatever *that* is) and the propaganda to which we are usually subjected.

I do want to give a shout out to the late Professor Howard Zinn, whose book *A People's History of the United States* has provided a lot of fodder for my ruminations, research, and exhortations. I am grateful my daughter Lena gave me that book as a birthday gift a few years ago. I learned so much more about my country from that book than I ever did in the history courses (I suppose calling these classes "history lite" would be more appropriate) that I took in high school or college.

I am sincerely troubled by all the drama and vitriol that continues to revolve around the issue that we call race. Inasmuch as, genetically, there is only one human race—*Homo sapiens*—I will make every concerted effort to use the term *ethnicity* whenever I am referring to different ethnic groups of people. We seem to keep making the same assumptions and repeating the same patterns and the same mistakes. I fervently believe that many of us continue to let the false issue of race color our worldview (pun intended), (mis)inform our decisions, and keep us in a place where people of common interests allow themselves to be kept separate because of the skin they're in. Self-preservation demands that we stop falling for the same misrepresentations and lies over and over again and take a deeper look at our common interests. These common interests must then motivate and empower us to do and become something different and far better than we are now. "If we do what we've always done, we'll continue to get what we've always gotten." Family, it's time to stop falling for the okeydoke! (For my purposes, "okeydoke" is something that is absurd and ridiculous or something that is designed to swindle or deceive).

Ground Rules:

1) In the following pages, other than when I am quoting the work of others, I will use the term *ethnicity* instead of *race*. There is only one race—the human race (see chapter 2, "The Skin I'm In").

2) If I am referring to the disaffection between ethnic groups, I will often use the term *ethnicism,* instead of *racism.* See rule 1.

3) Many of the things attributed to race are more often matters of the economic class that people are born into and that often hold them fast all of their lives. I will use the term *classism* or *classist* when referring to that dynamic.

4) Unless quoting directly from another source, I will almost always refer to black people as brown. Why? Because it's true. In my life, I have seen *very* few black people (people whose skin color is actually black), but I have seen a whole heap of brown ones! In my desire for more literal accuracy in that regard, I will usually not use the widely used and accepted term, but the more accurate one.

Some might ask, well, how do we distinguish between Latinos—those we currently call *brown* from African Americans? The answer is simple: refer to them as *Latino* and *African American*. In truth, most people on the planet are various shades of brown, ranging from beige to dark chocolate. I am not interested in being limited by or continuing to propagate the well-established lines of descriptive division that help to keep us separated.

5) Finally, throughout the book, especially when commenting on work that I am quoting or referencing, I will often highlight a significant portion of the quoted text by italicizing it. These notations are the added emphasis being applied to, what I feel are, the most significant points being made by the writer. I will also use them on occasion in my own writing for added emphasis, which may include a [bracketed comment] in the midst of a quote, especially an extensive one.

You have your ground rules!

Chapter 1

IN MY BEGINNING

*I come from people who refused to let their
captive beginnings hold the remainder
of their lives in chains.*

I am the great-grandson of people who were enslaved here in the United States. Victims of, as former secretary of state Condoleezza Rice put it, "America's birth defect." Nevertheless, within a few short years after the emancipation, a maternal great-grandfather was a landowner and farmer. He had diligently pursued education in order to read and compute. Ultimately, "Professor" Andrew Jackson Johnson (1859–1930) became the principal of the General School (for colored children) in Aberdeen, Mississippi. A maternal great-great-grandmother, Mahala Whitfield (1842–1921), was a highly respected and much-sought-after midwife for both colored and white folks. By the early part of the twentieth century, my grandmother (and Mahala's granddaughter), Josephine Brooks Johnson, after completing high school, attended Rust College in Holly Springs, Mississippi. Less than twenty years into the new century, a mere generation after slavery, "Gramma" had attended college and then returned to Aberdeen to teach.

According to an oral history taken from my paternal grandmother's older brother, my paternal great-grandfather escaped slavery as a boy and found his way into service as a mess boy for Union troops stationed in Maryland. He had the good fortune of

1

having the mother of the officer he served tell her son that she wanted to take the young man, in whom she sensed a keen intelligence, back to Pennsylvania with her to live with her family and receive an education. When he returned to the South after the end of the Civil War, young George Allen Mebane (1850–1900) had received his education. According to my father and aunt, he may have even spent some time in college in Pennsylvania before returning to North Carolina to find his parents and family. Within a few years, he had become a publisher, businessman, educator, state senator, congressional candidate, and registrar of deeds during the Reconstruction Era.

I suspect that the stuff and motivation that made him aspire to break chains and exceed limits might have come from his ancestral background. His grandfather, whose name I do not know, was supposed to have been an African prince who was kidnapped and sold into enslavement on American shores. He was the father of Allen Capehart (on the Capehart plantation in North Carolina) who was my great-great-grandfather.

> The effort to steal the soul and humanity from the stolen Africans was unsuccessful!

(They became "Mebane" when given, as a wedding gift, when their Capehart daughter married into the Mebane family). *Senator Mebane's story is a sign to me that the effort to steal the soul and humanity from the stolen Africans was unsuccessful!* In fact, science has recently allowed me to recover some family heritage information that had been lost to my family as a result of their former stolen status. As a result of the fine work of the good people at African Ancestry (www. AfricanAncestry.com), I have learned that I am descended from the Temne of Sierra Leone on Mom's side and the Mbundu of Angola on Dad's side. I *treasure* this new knowledge about my roots far beyond plantations in Mississippi and North Carolina!

From these achievers, people who refused to let their captive beginnings hold the remainder of their lives in chains, have come generations of educators, including my dad, who went from delivering mail to being a teacher, counselor, assistant principal, and principal, and Mom, who was an English teacher par excellence and also served as an administrator in the central office for DC Public Schools. (At age ninety-two, she edited this book.) Also in the family are persons who served in the military in every conflict from the Spanish-American War, both world wars, Korea, Vietnam, and the Gulf War era). Our family has produced ministers and pastors, and within my generation and the next, we have a budding opera singer, musicians, a lawyer, entrepreneurs, Peace Corps volunteers, reporters and news anchors, computer wizards, and more.

Whereas in some families, college was an *aspiration*, in mine, it was an *expectation*. Before I was even born, it was expected that if I possessed even a modicum of intellectual ability, I would have the opportunity to go to college if I applied myself to make it happen. My parents paid for my secondary and undergraduate education, and I paid for seminary. This is not intended to brag on myself or my family. It is merely intended to illustrate that I am the beneficiary of the choices of my foreparents that led to considerable opportunities. Children born into families where education was not valued and insisted upon had a steeper hill to climb and more obstacles to face. For those children, an advanced education wouldn't necessarily be impossible, but it would be considerably more challenging. We have simply tried to do as much as we could with the opportunities that presented themselves. When opportunities didn't come knocking, we would persevere and overcome the obstacles; we let nothing come between us and our goals. But I use my family as a point of illustration that after the period of enslavement, our foreparents elevated themselves from their illegal and inhumane enslavement and humble beginnings to make contributions. As my fraternity Kappa Alpha Psi likes to say, they were driven "to achieve in every field of human endeavor."

Another new thing that has occurred in the family is that over the past two generations, the social interactions have included a much broader array of people. Some cousins, in both my immediate and extended families, have found spouses from outside of our once-segregated community. A sign of how truly interwoven our family is becoming with other branches of the human family, my biracial younger cousin married a woman from India in a Hindu ceremony. The multiethnic and multicultural flavor of their wonderful, three-day celebration gives me hope that the next generations may yet escape and circumvent the bile and disconnection of their foreparents and lead our world to a more united place in the decades and centuries to come. All of this speaks to a fundamental aspect of our human nature to connect with other people—other members of the human race—without limits, aspersions, or judgments, based solely upon who we are—and nothing else.

I feel compelled to comment here about the conundrum that children from multiethnic relationships face. As long as I can remember, it felt as if persons of diverse heritage were almost compelled by their peers to *choose* which segment of their being they preferred. "Which portion of your ethnic heritage do you affirm, your mama's or your daddy's?" or "Which side of your family tree do you value more?" Think about that for a moment: these children were expected to choose which portion of themselves to own and which portion to disavow. To disown seems a bit strong; do we then say *deemphasize*? They are asked to decide which portion of themselves is more important, which side they prefer. Inasmuch as those individuals could not exist as they are without *all* of the ethnic ingredients within them comprising the whole of who they are, that's a ridiculous question and concept. Yet I can remember that "mixed" African American kids were once considered sellouts (or worse) if they did not wholly embrace the brown portion of who they were and to (at least appear to) dismiss the white portion.

To highlight this intrapersonal warfare (within oneself) the world imposes on these children, I share this story of twins born to a couple in the United Kingdom in 2006. Both the father and mother of these twin girls, Remi and Kylie, were the products of a white mother and a brown father. They gave birth to fraternal twin girls. One sister had white skin and blonde hair, and the other had brown skin and dark hair. The explanation given was that the genetic material for the fertilized egg that resulted in the white twin largely came from each parent's white side of the family tree, while the genetic material for the fertilized egg that led to the brown daughter largely came from each parent's brown side of the family.

Here's where it gets stupid: the media attention and commentary about this rare birth refers to these twins being of "different races." So twins conceived from the *same* mother and father, who shared the *same* womb from conception, and were born two minutes apart are now from different races? Really? According to society's shopworn use of the word *race*, it would imply that they are wholly other from one another. That is how tortured and insistent the race line of thinking is that it would try to "otherize" twins at birth, based on the color of their skin.

There were no interracial marriages in my immediate family before the 1980s. With parents born before the Great Depression, how did I find my way out of the box that has kept us separated from one another for such a long time? While my family has done well, in spite of the systemic obstacles, we have not been immune to the whims of apartheid in America. In theory, I should be as wary and pre-prejudiced (meaning folks who don't look like me that would be "guilty until proven innocent") in my dealings with others, as many with a family history common to mine often are. I believe there were two factors that allowed me to look past the superficial and try to deal with each individual for who they really are (or presented themselves to be), rather than simply hunkering down in my own assumptions and generational resentments, with the expectation that I would refuse to engage with people different than myself.

First, the neighborhood in which I grew up was diverse: across the alley, one family of neighbors was Jewish, and their household included a Holocaust survivor; next door, an educator and Realtor from Alabama lived; across the alley, an African ambassador's family resided; down the alley, our neighborhood had a touch of Creole from Louisiana; across the alley, we had a Jamaican neighbor; up the street, our orthodox Jews taught us why they would never drive on their Shabbat (Sabbath/Saturdays), but would walk the seven blocks to their synagogue; in the next block was an interracial couple whose children "looked white." Their eldest son was one of my best friends as we grew up. I was surrounded by the diverse expression of the human family. The same could be said for my schooling. Other than nursery school and third and fourth grade, I was always in diverse environments, from elementary school through seminary. Sometimes African Americans were in the majority, but usually we were not. As a result, it helped to demystify *others* (by which I mean people not exactly like me), and this allowed me to choose friendships based solely on the substance and quality of the person, and more importantly, based upon how they treated and regarded me. No relationships are perfect, but each stood or stumbled under its own weight and without preconceived notions or assumptions.

As I look back on it, I did have what I felt then was an odd experience during my first year in high school. In 1972, St. John's College High School had grades eight to twelve. My first year there, as an eighth grader, I formed a fast friendship with another eighth grader, a classmate of Greek heritage named George. At first, we hung around with each other all the time. At lunch, we sat at the same table. In classes, we usually sat near one another and chatted. Well, before the first marking period was completed, his older brother, also a student at the school, and some of the older African American students let us both know that we weren't playing by the rules and that we needed to spend our friendship/social time with people who looked like we did. Under the pressure of upperclassmen, our young friendship quickly ended. We remained cordial, but the budding friendship had been effectively snuffed out. I didn't understand it then, and honestly, it still kind of annoys me now, more than forty years later. What was the harm? Why couldn't the older and more cynical kids have just left us alone to find our own way? It's not as if we were slighting and not dealing with our own; we simply had found a friend in an other.

Second, and much more profoundly, was a life- and perspective-changing experience in my first pastoral appointment. On January 1, 1990, I was assigned as the pastor of the First United Methodist Church, Bradbury Heights in Washington, DC (FCBH). I was the first African American pastor in their 160-year history! On the surface, this appointment looked as if it might be doomed to fail at the outset. Here I was, thirty years old, still in seminary and wholly inexperienced in pastoral ministry, and certainly inexperienced in facilitating any shifts on ages-old cultural norms. I was an African American man born and reared in Washington, DC, who was sent to serve as pastor of an elderly majority white, *southern* white congregation. If there was ever something that *wasn't* going to work, this was probably it. But in the six and a half years I served as their pastor, the Lord knit us together like family. Were there a few bumps in the road? Of course. I'll admit that many of those bumps were due to my being a rookie pastor. But my experience there was a tremendous growth experience. This is where I learned about *the fundamental sameness of human beings.* Irrespective of our place of birth or the color of our skin, we all experienced the joys, pains, heartbreaks, and victories of life in largely the same way. Life circumstances were no respecter of person.

I remember the first funeral service I had to conduct. I had been at FCBH about a year, and the daughter of one of our older members died. Sister Sophie Brown is one of the sweetest people I've ever known, a truly genuine Christian. What you saw was what you got! Whenever I get to heaven, she's one of the first people I hope to see. I had never met her daughter before; she didn't attend the church. When I went to visit her in the hospital, she was in critical condition and unable to respond, so I never had a chance to get to know her. When she died, Sophie asked me to preside over her daughter's service and preach the eulogy. Again, this was my *first* funeral service.

Before I tell you about what happened when I arrived at the funeral home to conduct the service, I want to tell you about an interesting cultural difference I discovered. While white folks (even those who had been active church members) often held their funerals at the funeral home, black folks (even those who had not been active church members) almost always had their funerals—also known as "homegoings"—*in* a church.

On that day, Sophie greeted me and asked me how *I* was doing. Here she was preparing to bury her only daughter, and she was asking *me* how *I* am!

I told her, with no pretense or false bravado, "I'm nervous."

God bless her, her response was, "Well, this will be good practice for you, then!"

Who says that? When people are in pain, most of them are, understandably, too caught up in their own grief to concern themselves with what others are going through. Sophie was one of the most truly Christian and loving people I have ever met, and she elevated me with her loving presence my entire time at FCBH.

While at FCBH, I encountered a church family that really functioned as a family. You had people of one ethnicity showing genuine care and concern for people of another ethnicity. Whether it was shoveling an elder's walk in the winter, providing a ride to the store or the doctor, or visiting the sick or homebound, this congregation functioned as a community. I do remember, with amusement, what happened when I tried to spice up the music a little. One of the white members who sang in the choir stated, somewhat matter-of-factly, that "The people who have joined this church joined it *as it was*." Translation: "The African Americans who are members here joined the church knowing what our particular style of worship and music is." I had never even processed that thought paradigm before. Rather than taking it as a challenge, I received it as useful information from someone helping me not to shoot myself in the foot. Over time, we did bring more variety into the music ministry (though not so much until the retirement of the long-serving organist, a skilled musician who played *everything* fast); but I always kept that member's observation in mind.

The congregation, which had a few younger families, was very welcoming to me and my young family. My son, Drew, was three and a half when we arrived at FCBH. My daughter Lena was a month shy of her second birthday. On the occasions when she could wrest free of her mother, she would come running down the aisle to the front of the church because, well, that's where Daddy was. I would pick her up and keep preaching! In spite of our different cultural and ethnic histories, the church embraced us and seemed to enjoy having a pastor with young children for the first time in a number of years.

One day, one of our elder members was talking with my wife about her love of dancing. She spoke with such passion of how she used to dance all the time when she was younger. When speaking about her roots, Rose then described herself: "I'm just a Georgia cracker." She didn't say it with a trace of irony or bitterness. It did not seem to be a loaded word to her at all. Out of her milieu and personal history, it was simply descriptive.

In the movie *Remember the Titans,* a young white player named Louis Lastik, a member of a naval family that was new to the area, transferred into T.C. Williams High School in Alexandria, Virginia. Louis tried out for the football team. He was unaware, and didn't seem to care, that the school was in the midst its first year of an unsettling integration forced upon it by the courts and the changing times. He was even chided by his teammates, both white and black, during football camp, when he sat to eat lunch at the "black table."

The black players asked him, "What are you doing *here*, man?"

"Eating lunch," he replied.

"I see you eating lunch. But why are you eating over *here*? Why don't you go eat with *your* people?"

Louie replied, "Man, I don't have any people. I'm just with everybody."

This interaction brought him to the head coach's attention, and Coach Norman Boone asked him about his plans after high school. "Do you want to go to college?"

Louis said that he did not.

The coach pressed him. "If you don't go to college, it's not because you're not qualified. So I want you to bring me your test scores at the end of every week, and we'll go over them together."

(Now, I imagine right about now you're asking yourself, "Why is Tillett going on and on about this movie? What does that have to do with the okeydoke and Georgia crackers?" I'm so glad you asked. Read on.)

A little later, we see Louie in his room with his roommate, the African American quarterback of the team everyone called "Rev." Rev is trying to encourage Louie to consider and pursue the possibility of college.

Here's what Louie said about himself. "Nobody from my family ever went to no college."

Rev said, "I'll tutor you, Louie."

Louie emphatically said, "I'm white trash. I ain't gonna get no C-plus grades. I'm just down-home, no-good, never-going-to-college white trash!"

I don't know where Louie's family was from, but I suspect they're probably from somewhere in the South. The cultural expectations (or lack thereof) were so deeply ingrained, that this teenager describes himself as "just down-home, no good, never-going-to-college white trash." He didn't seem to be especially upset to say that about himself (and by implication, his whole family). Instead, he seemed more upset that his coach and now his new friend and quarterback were trying to push him through the glass ceiling imposed upon his family, simply because of the circumstances of his birth. There *must* be a disease in us as a society that would have a teenager, with his whole life before him stating, emphatically, that he is unfit to even *aspire* to do better than those who had come before him.

Let's fast-forward to a scene near the end of the movie. We rejoin the story in the locker room the night of the Virginia state championship game. As the locker room clears out for pregame warm-ups, Coach Boone asks Louis if he's okay. The young player emotionally hugs the coach and says, "I'm eligible."

With help from his African American coach and teammate, this poor white kid was now eligible to go to college. He did go to Austin Peay State, where he played for four years. In the epilogue to the movie, we learn that Louis is a successful businessman. All of this happened because people were willing to avoid classist behavior and see beyond his socioeconomic status, the educational history of his family, or any other artificial hindrance. They supported him and encouraged him—and he thrived.

The reason I bring up this film, based on the *true* story of the T.C. Williams football team in 1971, is to highlight the young man's self-description. He saw himself as "poor white trash." My church member, Rose, referred to herself as "just a Georgia cracker." Both of these statements are illustrative of the stratification that we have allowed to be forced upon us in this country. I remember hearing my grandmother, who was born in 1894 and reared in Aberdeen, Mississippi, refer to poor whites as trash. She didn't say it vindictively or in response to some insult. It was just something she learned in her youth that she was repeating to her grandson, in a conversation, seven decades later. It was a descriptive, dare I say, catch-all term, used to refer to whites who had less financial viability and education than others. But what human being willingly and habitually calls other people, or allows himself to be called trash or cracker? What kind of classist system is in place where those words are understood to be an acceptable thing to say when talking about another human being? I won't even get into the litany of names historically used for people of color.

There is a deep-seated illness—a disease—that permits and allows human beings to call and accept being called such names. More than that, it also allows for them to accept a certain place in life. It forces them to accept as normal a stratification that would entomb for life persons born into certain circumstances from which they can never escape—unless by grit and good fortune, they shatter societal expectations and succeed. In the context of the African American community, and especially those whose foreparents were enslaved, it all takes us back to that original "birth defect."

The thing about birth defects is that while some are irreversible, others can be overcome with surgeries, therapy, and time. In order for us to overcome our unhealthy beginnings, we must make dedicated and unswerving effort to move away from our infirmity or illness and head toward wellness. Either we want to be well or we do not. Either we are committed to being well or we are not. Either we will continue to accept being seen and referred to as a cracker or as poor white trash or a nigger (or nigga) *or we will not!*

It is okeydoke like this that sets the stage for unwarranted resentments between people with similar socioeconomic status, who have far more in common than they realize or are willing to acknowledge or accept. They have been acculturated, almost from birth, to see anyone who is *other* as wholly foreign, threatening, and intrinsically less valuable. Who benefits from this disconnection? Who is harmed? I'm so glad you asked. Keep reading.

Epilogue on Sister Rose: In July of 1996, I was appointed to serve a congregation in Baltimore. A short while later, Rose was mugged by some young punk who decided to rob a woman in her eighties. When she fell to the ground, she broke her hip. Her daughters then moved her out of her home of many years to live with one of them in another part of the state. When she died a few years later, these four daughters—who could have held resentment against anyone whose skin was brown, because of what happened to their mother—sought

11

me out to preach their mother's eulogy. The "Georgia cracker's" daughters, tracked down the black guy from Washington, DC, to share in one of their family's most intimate moments—the funeral service for their mom. In a world torn with strife—sometimes manufactured, centuries-old strife—some wonderful things can happen if we are willing to emerge from our separate corners, engage one another, and do the hard work of relationship building for our mutual benefit.

Chapter 2

THE SKIN I'M IN

*The scientific community, using the most
advanced tools available, has determined that the whole
social concept of race is "a bogus idea."*

T he lie of race has been an impediment to the United States fully becoming the "more perfect union" it lifted up as a goal in its founding documents. In the second paragraph, the Declaration of Independence states, "We hold these truths to be self-evident, that all men are, created equal, that they endowed by their Creator with certain unalienable Rights, that among these are Life, Liberty and the pursuit of Happiness." Yet these self-evident truths have often been crushed to earth by divisions among ethnic groups sown for the economic and social convenience of others. But before I get into the real okeydoke of the matter, let's see what science has to say about this thing we routinely and casually call race. Because of the advancements of science, the twenty-first century has provided new information. Some of it has emanated from the Human Genome Project, whose scientists have sought to map out our genetic code to learn more about human beings at a genetic level.

According to the popular and widely accepted narrative, there are three races of people on the planet. Mongoloid (people of Asian descent), Caucasoid/Caucasian (white people), and Africoid (people of African descent). Over the years, people with more of a socioeconomic agenda, under the guise of (fake) science, have

13

erected barriers between members of the human family based on the false notion of race. I state emphatically something that is not a new truth, yet it continues to be widely ignored because there is no continuing financial advantage to the wealthy or the business community in this truth: *There is only one race, the human race. There are ethnicities within the human family—branches of the family, if you will—but to assert that white people or brown people*

> **T**here is only one race, the human race.

or so-called yellow or red people are so different genetically as to actually be another race of human being is absurd and is not supported by science. By way of example, let's look at dogs. No one would ever assert that a poodle, a collie, or a German shepherd is a different level of dog—a different race from each other or a different scientific classification. They are all dogs, just a different breed of dog. In the same way, a Haitian, a Dane, an Australian Aborigine, and a Korean are not different levels of human being. They are not different races. They are simply of a different ethnicity, a different expression of the human family as a result of geography and reproduction opportunities.

I will now quote extensively (with comment) from several studies about the genetic makeup of the human family. Here is what science has to say about this whole race thing.

In her August 22, 2000, *New York Times* article "Do Races Differ? Not Really, Genes Show," Natalie Angier writes the following.

> Scientists have long suspected that the racial categories recognized by society are not reflected on the genetic level. But the more closely that researchers examine the human genome—the complement of genetic material encased in the heart of almost every cell of the body—the more most of them are convinced that the standard labels used to distinguish people by race have little or no biological meaning.

They say that while it may seem easy to tell at a glance whether a person is Caucasian, African, or Asian, the ease dissolves when one probes beneath surface characteristics and scans the genome for DNA hallmarks of race.

As it turns out, scientists say, the human species is so evolutionarily young, and its migratory patterns so wide, restless and rococo (defined as *"excessively ornate or intricate, often used with mild disdain to describe the overly elaborate"*), that it has simply not had a chance to divide itself into separate biological groups or "races" in any but the most superficial ways.

"Race is a social concept, not a scientific one," said Dr. J. Craig Venter, head of the Celera

Race is a social concept, not a scientific one

Genomics Corporation in Rockville, Md. "We all evolved in the last 100,000 years from the same small number of tribes that migrated out of Africa and colonized the world." [We *all* migrated out of Africa— we have a common origin, so how could we possibly be a different race or species?]

Dr. Venter and scientists at the National Institutes of Health recently announced that they had put together a draft of the entire sequence of the human genome, and the researchers had unanimously declared, there is only one race—the human race. [So, in spite of whatever we heard at the kitchen table, in church, in school, or on the street, some of the finest scientific minds in the world have declared that, based on the scientifically verifiable *reality* of our human genome,

15

we are all one race—the human race.] (*Definition: A genome is an organism's complete set of DNA, including all of its genes. Each genome contains all of the information needed to build and maintain that organism. In humans, a copy of the entire genome — more than 3 billion DNA base pairs — is contained in all cells that have a nucleus.*)

Dr. Venter and other researchers say that those traits most commonly used to distinguish one race from another, like skin and eye color, hair texture, or the shape and width of the nose, are traits controlled by a relatively few number of genes, and thus have been able to change rapidly in response to extreme environmental pressures during the short course of the history of *Homo sapiens*. [Some of the most obvious variances in our external appearance are things that have changed rapidly in response to one's environment.]

And so equatorial populations evolved dark skin, presumably to protect against ultraviolet radiation, while people in northern latitudes evolved pale skin, the better to produce vitamin D from pale sunlight. [Again, as an adaptation to one's environment.]

"If you ask what percentage of your genes is reflected in your external appearance, the basis by which we talk about race, the answer seems to be in the range of .01 percent," said Dr. Harold P. Freeman, the chief executive, president, and director of surgery at North General Hospital in Manhattan, who has studied the issue of biology and race. "This is a very, very minimal reflection of your genetic makeup." [About one-tenth of 1 percent of our DNA determines these external differences; thus, we are 99.9 percent the same. How did such a small factor in our human composition become *the* driving force in centuries of mistreatment between one group, subset, tribe, ethnicity, and another? What else is at play here? The following chapters will provide some answers.]

By contrast with the tiny number of genes that make some people dark-skinned and doe-eyed, and others as pale as napkins, scientists say that traits like intelligence, artistic talent, and social skills are likely to be shaped by thousands, if not tens of thousands, of the 80,000 or so genes in the human genome, all working in complex combinatorial fashion.

The possibility of such gene networks shifting their interrelationships wholesale in the course of humanity's brief foray across the globe and being skewed in significant ways according to race is "a bogus idea," said Dr. Aravinda Chakravarti, a geneticist at Case Western University in Cleveland [Ohio]. "The differences that we see in skin color do not translate into widespread biological differences that are unique to groups."

Dr. Eric S. Lander, a genome expert at the Whitehead Institute in Cambridge, Massachusetts, says "There's no scientific evidence to support substantial differences between groups," he said, "and the tremendous burden of proof goes to anyone who wants to assert those differences." [If one wishes to assert these differences, one should be able to definitively and empirically prove it. It is more than simply a matter of opinion, custom, or tradition.]

Although research into the structure and sequence of the human genome is in its infancy, geneticists have pieced together a rough outline of human genomic history, variously called the "Out of Africa" or "Evolutionary Eve" hypothesis.

By this theory, modern *Homo sapiens* originated in Africa between 200,000 and 100,000 years ago, at which point a relatively small number of them, maybe 10,000 or so, began migrating into the Middle East, Europe, Asia, and across the Bering land mass into the Americas.

Since the African emigrations began, a mere 7,000 generations have passed. And because the founding population of emigres was small, it could only take so much genetic variation with it. As a result of that combination—a limited "founder population" [quotation marks added] and a short time since dispersal—humans are strikingly homogeneous, differing from one another only once in a thousand subunits of the genome.

"We are a small population grown large in the blink of an eye," Dr. Lander said. "We are a little village that's grown all over the world, and we retain the genetic variation seen in that little village." [We all came from the continent of Africa and retain the same genetic information millennia later.]

(Further), the citizens of any given village in the world, whether in Scotland or Tanzania, hold 90 percent of the genetic variability that humanity has to offer. [No matter where you are in the world, you hold, within your DNA, 90 percent of the possible genetic variations that can be found anywhere else on the planet.]

A few group differences are more than skin deep. Among the most famous examples are the elevated rates of sickle-cell anemia among African Americans, and of beta-thalassemia, another hemoglobin disorder, among those of Mediterranean heritage. Both traits evolved to help the ancestors of these groups resist malaria infection, but both prove lethal when inherited in a double dose [from both parents].

Another cause of group differences is the so-called "founder effect." In such cases, the high prevalence of an unusual condition in a population can be traced to a founding ancestor who happened to carry a novel mutation into the region. *Over many generations of comparative isolation and inbreeding, the community, like it or not, became "enriched" with the founder's disorder.* The founder effect explains the high incidence of Huntington's neurodegenerative disease in the Lake Maracaibo region of Venezuela, and of Tay-Sachs disease among Ashkenazi Jews. [Essentially, the *absence of genetic diversity* in a population can create an environment where rare diseases become prominent in a fairly isolated or insular population.]

Dr. Sonia S. Anand, an assistant professor of medicine at McMaster University in Ontario, proposed that clinicians think about ethnicity rather than race when seeking clues to how disease patterns differ from one group to the next.

"Ethnicity is a broad concept that encompasses both genetics and culture," Dr. Anand said. "Thinking about ethnicity is a way to bring together questions

19

of a person's biology, lifestyle, diet, rather than just focusing on race. [Ethnicity is determined by *how* we live and *where* we live.] Ethnicity is about phenotype (defined as, *the observable physical or biochemical characteristics of an organism, as determined by both genetic makeup and environmental influences. The expression of a specific trait, such as stature or blood type, based on genetic and environmental influences*), and genotype (defined as, *the genotype is the part (DNA sequence) of the genetic makeup of a cell, and therefore of an organism or individual, which determines a specific characteristic (phenotype) of that cell/organism/individual*), and, if you define the terms of your study, it allows you to look at differences between groups in a valid way."

[Again, the phenotype is observable or biochemical characteristics. The genotype is the DNA sequence at the cellular level that determines the phenotype.]

Therefore, the scientific community, using the most advanced tools available, has determined that the whole social concept of race is "a bogus idea." Ethnicity is real, but we are all fruit from the same tree, fundamentally the same at the genetic level. Our most prominent differences are the result of environment, over the course of time (e.g., levels of melanin in the skin), culture and exposure (or lack thereof) to other cultures/ethnic groups for the purpose of interaction (not domination), mating, and so on.

> **T**he scientific community, using the most advanced tools available, has determined that the whole social concept of race is "a bogus idea."

I would also make the observation that the culture from whence you came might give you more cultural similarities with persons of a different ethnicity who grew up near you than with a person of the same ethnicity from another part of the country. For example, there are some things particularly prevalent in southern culture (diet, idioms, customs) that would cause a white person and a brown person from, say, Mississippi to have more in common with each other than either might have with a corresponding white or brown person from Massachusetts. The forces of ethnicism in American culture would try to force the people of the same ethnicity into an expected alliance with one another, even though they might be more kindred with the folks from the same part of the country from a different ethnic background.

On the topic of race, Author Kenan Malik made these observations:

> Why is the character of race in scientific research so ambiguous? Because race is a social category but one which can have biological consequences. There is no such thing as a "natural" human population. Migration; intermarriage; war and conquest; forced assimilation; voluntary embrace of new or multiple identities whether religious, cultural, national, ethnic, or racial; any number of social, economic, religious, and other barriers to interaction (and hence to reproduction); social rules for defining populations such as the "one drop rule" in America—these and many social other factors impact upon the character of a group and transform its genetic profile. That is why racial categories are so difficult to define scientifically. [There are so many factors that have contributed to why and how we are clustered where we are and with whom. However, none of those factors are foundationally genetic in nature.]

The inimitable Dr. Albert Einstein wrote a short article on the topic of race in 1946 entitled "The Negro Question." I encourage you to look this up online and read the entire essay yourself.

Here are his observations. I'm sure they were the unwelcome observations of an outsider to many here in the United States, yet because of his standing in the world (and his enduring status as one of the greatest minds in the history of the world), he could not and cannot be completely or easily dismissed. He begins by confessing that he has only lived in the United States for ten years and understands that his observations, as a newcomer, may be unwelcome. He then goes on to suggest that newcomers may be able to see some things more readily than some who have grown up in that particular environment, as their familiarity may lead them to take many things for granted. He suggests his outsider's perspective may actually prove useful to those willing to receive what he has to say.

While he may be a relatively new arrival, he continues, Einstein states that he has a special devotion to and appreciation and affection for our country and our democracy. He then addresses some of the unique and powerful affirmations of personhood and liberty contained in our founding documents, where there is no expectation that any person "humble himself" before any other individual, irrespective of whatever advantages they may enjoy due to the circumstances of their birth or their wealth. Dr. Einstein then points out the obvious (to him) disconnect between those fine words and the reality under which US citizens of African descent were forced to live: "There is, however, a somber point in the social outlook of Americans. Their sense of equality and human dignity is mainly limited to men of white skins."

As a Jew who escaped from Europe ahead of Nazi atrocities, he concedes that he is quite conscious and sensitive to the mistreatment of a people solely because of personal characteristics over which they have no control. He refused to be complicit in the mistreatment of Negroes by not speaking out. He then plainly states the obvious about this shameful and regrettable situation: "Your ancestors dragged these black people from their homes by force; and in the white man's quest for wealth and an easy life, they have been ruthlessly suppressed and exploited, degraded into slavery. The modern prejudice against Negroes is the result of the desire to maintain this unworthy condition."

Einstein then makes a comparison between the ancient Greeks, who also had slaves they had captured in war, in comparison to slavery in the United States. While there was often no "racial" difference between the Greeks and their captors, they still felt compelled to insist that their slaves were inferior and so, were being rightfully deprived of their liberty and their personhood. Aristotle, considered one of the most astute thinkers in the history of the world, nevertheless ceded some of his humanity and his logic by agreeing with and affirming this mistreatment of fellow human beings. Intellect is not the same as wisdom or a viable perspective. Just because you're smart and think it, doesn't make it so!

Dr. Einstein then goes on to note that probably the most damaging and long-term effect that slavery had had on the *entire* country is the way it misinforms the children who grew up in those societies with such tortured logic about what Dr. Martin Luther King Jr. might call, "man's inhumanity to man." Children learn this errant worldview from their parents, and then, in turn, pass it along to their children and grandchildren as well. This self-perpetuating negative world view of "the other" can potentially toxify the whole society for generations to come. Einstein felt that kind of evil was unworthy for a country with the declared values and the rich promise of the United States.

In a commencement address at Rutgers University in 2015, Bill Nye "the Science Guy" put it this way:

> Along with the evidence of common sense, researchers have proven, scientifically, that humans are all one people ... The color of our ancestors' skin and ultimately my skin and your skin is a consequence of ultra-violet light, of latitude, and climate. Despite our recent sad conflicts here in the US, there really is no such thing as race. We are one species—each of us much, much more alike than different. We all come from Africa. We all are of the same star dust. We are all going to live and die on the same planet, a Pale Blue Dot in the vastness of space. We have to work together.

The World Is Flat

Some may question my use of such lengthy quotes and references from the work of others. First, there's no need to reinvent the wheel. If a credible scientist or institution has done the research and published their findings, it makes all the sense in the world to reference and quote their work, especially since many of my readers may not be familiar with the scientist's or institution's work. In addition, there were numerous other studies that I encountered doing my research. Much of it would not be called easy reading. Anyone with a desire and ability to sift through the minutia of research is free to do so.

The most important reason for quoting from the research of experts is simply to inform you, the reader, about the fallacious concept of race and how it has been used to harm and divide us to our own detriment. I use an expression in my preaching, *"When you know better, you have to do better!"* Once we know and are aware of the truth, it should compel us to respond to those truths with a transformed mind-set and behavior.

There was a time in the history of the world when it was believed that if one were on a ship and sailed too far off into the horizon, that ship would fall off the edge of the Earth because it was accepted as fact (common knowledge) that the world was flat. However, some brave seamen proved that assumption wrong when they got into their ships and kept sailing farther and farther into the horizon until they eventually realized that the world was indeed round, not flat. So, once they determined and could prove that the world was round, any further discussion based on the premise that the world was flat would be summarily dismissed as fiction, fable, and foolishness. Even for those who wanted to hold on to their old beliefs, legends, and stories told to them by their foreparents, those comfortable traditional stories could no longer hold up against the proven truth, the reality and the *fact* that the world is round.

In the same way, many of us have learned things in our families and communities of origin that are based upon the false concept of race. They do not have any basis in science or reality, but it's what we have always *heard*, and we are resistant (if not downright hostile) to scientific evidence that we are far more similar than we are different—over 99 percent similar, according to those who study these things.

In his *Time* magazine article entitled "Ignorance vs. Reason in the War on Education" (published September 23, 2015), Kareem Abdul-Jabbar, quoting the philosopher Sir Francis Bacon, said, "Almost 400 years ago, philosopher Francis Bacon wrote, 'The human understanding when it has once adopted an opinion ... draws all things else to support and agree with it. And though there be a greater number and weight of instances to be found on the other side, yet these it either neglects and despises.'"

Abdul-Jabbar, who in addition to being an NBA Hall of Famer, is also a brilliant man who is intellectually curious and exceptionally well-read, then went on to say:

> We seem hardwired to discard information that contradicts our beliefs. We have the Internet, the single most powerful information source and educational tool ever invented, but many of us use it only to confirm conclusions we didn't arrive at through examining evidence. *We go only to sites that agree with our position* in order to arm ourselves with snippets that we can use as ammunition against those who disagree with us.

The World Is Flat

This insightful article and analysis highlights one of our major challenges and failings as a largely uncurious people in 2016. Rather than taking advantage of the many resources at our fingertips (or at the very least, on a computer at the local library), people often do things the easy way. Rather than conduct some research on their own, they find talking heads *with whom they know in advance that they will already agree*, and take what they say as gospel, even if what has been said can be shown to be factually inaccurate, intentionally misrepresented, or contrived and inherently incorrect (perhaps even maliciously so). They are, in essence, continuing to maintain that the world is flat, even though it is demonstrably *not* flat!

"For the time will come when people will not put up with sound doctrine. Instead, to suit their own desires, they will gather around them a great number of 'teachers' [quotation marks added] to say what their itching ears want to hear. They will turn their ears away from the truth and turn aside to myths" (2 Timothy 4:3–4). Clearly this is not an entirely new phenomenon, as the almost two-thousand-year-old quote from the Bible and the four-century-old quote from Bacon indicate. Once we have adopted an opinion, however ill-informed it may be, we find as much as we can to agree with our erroneous position and neglect and derisively despise any demonstrable truths contrary to it.

The World Is Flat

Truth

Below are several quotes that speak to the need for truth to be spoken and received, irrespective of how inconvenient or discomfiting a truth it may be.

> Whoever is careless with the truth in small matters cannot be trusted with important matters.
> —Albert Einstein

> [Nuff said!]

> During times of universal deceit, telling the truth becomes a revolutionary act.
> —George Orwell

> [If telling the truth becomes an unusual and revolutionary act, it means lies are the *first* order of business and we are in serious trouble!]

There are two ways to be fooled. One is to believe what isn't true; the other is to refuse to believe what is true.

—Soren Kierkegaard

[The world is flat, no matter what!]

It's easier to fool people ... than to convince them they have been fooled.

—Mark Twain

[It is hard to undo the damage of the original fooling—to break through with correct information.]

Every violation of truth is not only a sort of suicide in the liar, but is a stab at the health of human society.

—Ralph Waldo Emerson

[The decline of truth, comity, and decency, one lie or half-truth at a time, is grievously wounding our society.]

Truth will ultimately prevail where there is pains to bring it to light.

—President George Washington

The truth is not for all men, but only for those who seek it.

—Ayn Rand

[*Both* Rand and Washington make it plain that truth will not just fall into our laps, but we must diligently seek it!]

All truth passes through three stages. First, it is ridiculed. Second, it is violently opposed. Third, it is accepted as being self-evident.

—Arthur Schopenhauer

[What do you mean "the world is round"? How ridiculous! Dammit, the world is flat! Well, of course the world is round. Who ever thought otherwise?]

Nothing in all the world is more dangerous than sincere ignorance and conscientious stupidity.

—Rev. Dr. Martin Luther King Jr.

[Some people are fully committed to their opinion, even if that opinion is nonsense.]

A fool finds no pleasure in understanding but delights in airing his own opinions.

—Proverbs 18:2

[Everybody talking doesn't know, may not be trying to know, and may not want you to know either!]

You are entitled to your own opinion, but you are not entitled to your own facts.

—Senator Daniel Patrick Moynihan

[We are all wrong every now and then. Admit it, learn and accept the truth and move on. Do not create or allege "facts" to advance your erroneous opinion.]

The truth is incontrovertible; malice may attack it, ignorance may deride it, but in the end, there it is.
— Winston Churchill

[The truth is truth, no matter how persistent and insistent her opponents may be.]

The discerning heart seeks knowledge, but the mouth of a fool feeds on folly.
— Proverbs 15:14

[There are those who actually seek knowledge, wherever it may lead, and those who do not!]

Truth crushed to earth shall rise again.
— William Cullen Bryant

[No lie can live forever.]

The truth has a power greater than a hundred lies.
— Dr. Howard Zinn

[Truth will ultimately be able to stand on its own solid foundation.]

You will know the truth, and the truth will make you free.
— Jesus (John 8:32)

[Nuff said!]

I close with these quotes from Rev. Dr. Martin Luther King's speech at the conclusion of the Selma-to-Montgomery March in 1965:

Our aim must never be to defeat or humiliate the white man, but to win his friendship and understanding. We must come to see that the end *we seek is a society at peace with itself, a society that can live with its conscience.* And that will be a day not of the white man, not of the black man. That will be the day of man as man.

Dr. King then asked, rhetorically, how long it would take for society to reach the necessary and honorable goal of human beings simply being able to live together, work together, and build a truly just society together. After some typical King-like oratorical artistry, he concluded:

I come to say to you this afternoon, however difficult the moment, however frustrating the hour, it will not be long, because "truth crushed to earth will rise again." How long? Not long, because "no lie can live forever." How long? Not long, because "you shall reap what you sow." How long? Not long, because the arc of the moral universe is long, but it bends toward justice.

Those persons who operate without any sense of what I would call a divine settling of accounts can continue to operate as if the bill for their malevolence, misfeasance, and malfeasance will never come due. Inasmuch as many who have intentionally manipulated systems to the disadvantage of poor people and brown people also claim to be people of faith, the fact that the arc of the moral universe bends toward justice should be very sobering.

It was Thomas Jefferson who said, "I tremble for my country when I reflect that God is just; that his justice cannot sleep forever." For those of us who believe that there is a God and that God is a God of justice and is the God of the oppressed (the numerous mentions in the Bible about the need for fairness and justice for widows, orphans and foreigners help to lay out that case), the bill for the hideous mistreatment of the poor will come due! God's justice cannot sleep forever. Perhaps we are being given a chance to get it right before it's too late. I pray that selfishness and greed don't cause us to miss that opportunity.

I reiterate a final point about the truth/science of our human and ethnic heritage: scientists who have forgotten more about the human genome than most of us will ever know have told us that race, a social and political construct (more on that later), does not exist in science or nature. When we continue to insist that human beings actually are different races, in effect we are saying that the world is flat. We will continue to maintain our opinion and position, facts and science be damned. We are "discarding information that contradicts our beliefs" and will, to our own detriment and that of the country we say we love, allow ourselves to be separated from people of common interest just because they may not look like us! Who does this benefit? I'm so glad you asked. Read on.

> Race, a social and political construct does not exist in science or nature.

Chapter 3

THE BIG LIE

I tremble for my country when I reflect that
God is just; that his justice cannot sleep forever.
— President Thomas Jefferson

I now return to Dr. King's speech, referenced in the previous chapter, given at the end of the historic march from Selma to Montgomery, Alabama, on March 25, 1965. In this portion of the speech, Dr. King addressed the insidious and manipulative history of racial animus. When you read these words, the tone might sound somewhat unfamiliar. The public presentation and understanding of Dr. King, the martyr, do not begin to capture the full essence of the pastoral voice of Reverend Dr. Martin Luther King Jr, the prophet. Those who are all well familiar with his "I Have a Dream" speech find great comfort and affirmation in those words. However, the role of a prophet is to not only "comfort the afflicted" but also to "afflict the comfortable." Indeed, even the first portion of the "Dream" speech is a political analysis and critique, but it is one that is seldom heard or remarked upon. Dr. King was not the comforting, mildly nonthreatening dreamer he has been comfortably portrayed as being (a fantasy we dutifully digest every Martin Luther King holiday and for Black History Month observances). If he had *only* been a dreamer, he might still be alive today.

With the world watching after the unspeakable violence against nonviolent protesters on Bloody Sunday, Dr. King used this occasion as a teachable moment to help everyone who tuned in to learn this history and the root causes of racism in the Jim Crow South. They were intentional with malice aforethought and were having devastating consequences on brown and white people alike. While the focus of the march had been to obtain the unfettered right to vote for all citizens of Alabama, there were other interrelated concerns as well.

See now the words of a prophet in his incisive critique of the nation he loves and the poisoned fruit of its "original sin/birth defect."

> King: Racial segregation as a way of life did not come about as a natural result of hatred between the races immediately after the Civil War. There were no laws segregating the races then.

Dr. King then referenced a book by historian C. Vann Woodward, *The Strange Career of Jim Crow,* which identified the political rationale and strategy for the separation of the races. Woodward noted that those who stood to benefit the most from the disconnection were the "Bourbon interests" of the late 1800s. "Bourbon Democrat" was a term used to refer to a conservative member of the Democratic Party. The term "Bourbon" was mostly used disparagingly by critics complaining of old-fashioned viewpoints. They represented business interests that generally supported the goals of the banks and railroads. These Bourbon Democrats did everything in their power to keep poor people of different ethnicities divided, in order to ensure that labor costs would be the cheapest in the nation.

King went on to explain:

> It was a simple thing to keep the poor white masses working for near-starvation wages in the years that followed the Civil War. Why, if the poor white plantation or mill worker became dissatisfied with his low wages, the plantation or mill owner would merely threaten to fire him and hire former Negro slaves and pay him even less. Thus, the southern wage level was kept almost unbearably low.

However, during this time period of intentionally manipulated animus between white people and brown people, the Populist Movement was born. Movement leaders began to show both the formerly enslaved Negroes and poor whites that their division was only working to the financial advantage of the Bourbon interests. As these formerly disparate communities began to coalesce into a united voting bloc, held together by their common needs and common interests, their coalition began to threaten a paradigm shift in the South that could drive the Bourbons and others from political power.

In response to this coming together of brown people and poor white people as a voting bloc, the entrenched business interests began to plant the seeds for a segregated society, which included denying those formerly enslaved their constitutionally granted right to vote. The business elite were especially concerned about the combined potential for the working poor to use the ballot to bring about changes that would require them to pay a fair wage, so it was imperative that Negroes and whites be kept separated at all costs!

> King: To meet this threat, the southern aristocracy began immediately to engineer this development of a segregated society ... Through their control of mass media, they revised the doctrine of white supremacy. They directed the placement on the books of the South of laws that made it a crime for Negroes and whites to come together as equals at any level.

These laws led to the crippling and eventual ending of the Populist Movement.

> King: If it may be said of the slavery era that the white man took the world and gave the Negro Jesus, then it may be said of the Reconstruction era that the Southern aristocracy took the world and gave the poor white man Jim Crow ... And when his wrinkled stomach cried out for the food that his empty pockets could not provide, he ate Jim Crow, a psychological

bird that told him that no matter how bad off he was, at least he was a white man, better than the black man. And he ate Jim Crow.

So even when hungry white children did not even have the basics of life, due to the depressed wages earned by their fathers, white supremacy could point to the Jim Crow signs on buses, in the streets, in stores and in other public accommodations so that, as Dr. King said, they "learned to feed upon Jim Crow, their last outpost of psychological oblivion." Sadly, this approach continued to flourish with working people working against their own self-interests to the advantage of entrenched business interests. Once the children became adults, they would dutifully pass down that ideology to their struggling families, as well, from generation to generation.

Dr. King concluded this economic history lesson by saying:

> The threat of the free exercise of the ballot by the Negro and the white masses ... resulted in the establishment of a segregated society. They segregated Southern money from the poor whites; they segregated Southern mores from the rich whites; they segregated Southern churches from Christianity; they segregated Southern minds from honest thinking; and they segregated the Negro from everything. That's what happened when the Negro and white masses of the South threatened to unite and build a great society.

The game of divide and conquer is not new. It is not even original. It is an ages-old ploy to keep people of like interests separated, so that the people who profit from their manipulated separation, *colored* most of all by greed, will keep right on profiting. By employing this deceptive strategy effectively, over and over again, poor white people have been repeatedly convinced that their struggles are the fault of brown people. They are powerless people being led to believe that their problems are being caused by *other* powerless people.

Thus, they misdirect their fire and blame and scapegoat people who could not truly influence their standard of living if they tried.

When asked why poor and middle-class whites vote against their own interests, President Lyndon Baines Johnson put it this way: "If you can convince the lowest white man he's better than the best colored man, he won't know you're picking his pocket. Hell, give him someone to look down on, and he'll empty his pockets for you."

> "If you can convince the lowest white man he's better than the best colored man, he won't know you're picking his pocket. Hell, give him someone to look down on, and he'll empty his pockets for you."

On February 3, 2014, an article appeared on the Political Blindspot website entitled "The Food Stamp Capital of the U.S. Is White and Republican." There are assumptions that are routinely made about who the beneficiaries are from public assistance. The information about the SNAP (Supplemental Nutrition Assistance Program, what was once known as food stamps) is especially, and I would suggest, *intentionally* misrepresented. The article presents data that informs us "the highest usage is *not* in Compton, Queens, nor the south side of Chicago." Rather it is from a county that is 99.22 percent white and 95 percent Republican—Owsley County, Kentucky. Owsley County has a population of around five thousand, and its median household income is the lowest in the nation (outside of the territory of Puerto Rico). This has been brought about, at least in part, by the decline of the industries upon which the residents of Owsley County used to depend: coal, lumber, and tobacco.

In 2010, Cale Turner, the county executive of Owsley County, was interviewed by ABC. In that interview, Turner observed that there was a high incidence of drug addiction that had accompanied the economic distress in Owsley. He said that the people with addictions often wound up in prison, due to the lack of effective treatment programs. It is a recurring problem that shows no signs of abating. So again, we see in Owsley County—as we have seen around the country—a willingness to warehouse and throw away people who have an illness called addiction, rather than provide effective treatment for their condition. The pattern and conundrum is the same that unless one has the resources to afford a treatment program or rehabilitation facility, jail often becomes a first option for addicts. For these economically suppressed addicts, no protections due to "affluenza" are available. There are no concerns about "not wanting to damage or hinder a person's future" due to an "unfortunate mistake" to keep them from imprisonment. Instead, it becomes "Go Directly To Jail. Do Not Pass Go. Do Not Collect $200!" I guess you should only have an illness in this country if you can afford it!

The greatest irony here, though, is that in spite of their deep-seated needs and the traditional opposition to public assistance by the Republican Party, the residents of Owsley County continue to vote Republican, even when it is the GOP who has slashed their benefits. The philosopher Rousseau said that "self-preservation is the first law of humanity." Apparently not when it comes to voting one's own self-interest.

The incorrect assumption about those who rely on food stamps in our nation is that the majority of persons receiving food stamps are brown people—African Americans and Hispanics. That is not true! A 2015 report by the US Census Bureau determined that approximately 52.2 million (or 21.3 percent) of the people in the United States participated in major means-tested government assistance programs each month in 2012. Participation rates were highest for Medicaid (15.3 percent) and the Supplemental Nutrition Assistance Program (SNAP), formerly known as the Food Stamp Program (13.4 percent). So *one in five Americans requires medical assistance or nutritional assistance to survive*. Meanwhile, 39.2 percent of children received some type of means-tested assistance. Almost four in ten children, *with no responsibility for the circumstances of their birth*, need federal assistance. **What politicians cynically presented to their undiscerning white constituents as public policy intended to keep brown people in line is really a war against poor people, a majority of whom are white!**

The level of education of people receiving public assistance reveals that 37.9 percent of people who did not graduate from high school received benefits, as did 21.6 percent of high school graduates and 9.6 percent of individuals with one or more years of college. The higher one's level of education, the lower the chances one will need public assistance to survive. The weakening of the nation's manufacturing sector also contributes to these figures as jobs that pay a living wage or better for the less educated have dwindled.

In a February 28, 2015, *Huffington Post* article entitled "Who Gets Food Stamps? White People, Mostly," the following data was shared:

> Nationally, *most of the people who receive benefits from the Supplemental Nutrition Assistance Program (SNAP) are white.* [Emphasis mine.] According to 2013 data from the U.S. Department of Agriculture, which administers the program, 40.2 percent of SNAP recipients are white, 25.7 percent are black, 10.3 percent are Hispanic, 2.1 percent are Asian, and 1.2 percent are Native American. Further, 44.8 percent of SNAP households have children, elderly, and/or disabled residents.

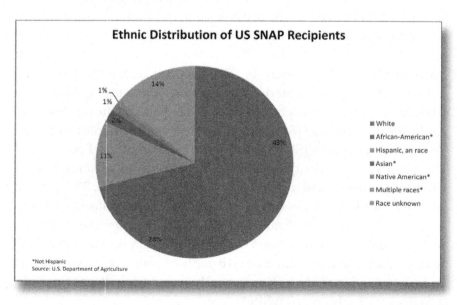

Children, the elderly, and the disabled are hardly lazy layabouts! It has been said, you can tell a lot about a society by how it treats its powerless, its young, its elderly, and its infirm. What does the obsession to cut benefits for these vulnerable populations say about the soul and character of our country? More specifically, what does it say about our legislators, who clearly do *not* represent us—and who certainly don't represent the poor?

> It has been said, you can tell a lot about a society by how it treats its powerless, its young, its elderly, and its infirm. What does the obsession to cut benefits for these vulnerable populations say about the soul and character of our country?

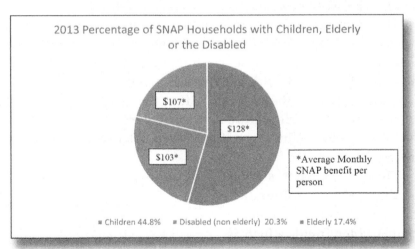

2013 Percentage of SNAP Households with Children, Elderly or the Disabled

$107*

$128*

$103*

*Average Monthly SNAP benefit per person

■ Children 44.8%   ■ Disabled (non elderly) 20.3%   ■ Elderly 17.4%

Let's go back to Owsley County, Kentucky, for a minute. That community is 99.22 percent white and 95 percent Republican. The loss of the manufacturing base in this community has created an environment where no jobs leads to despair and the resulting associated ills of drug use. This, in turn, has increased our nation's "incarcerate first" modus operandi resulting in people who are addicted to drugs being sent to prison rather than to treatment facilities. Well, at least the Department of Corrections is able to provide *some* jobs! Poor people who no longer work in manufacturing can get jobs watching other poor people with no jobs (and many with addiction problems) as they waste away in jail. If there was ever a more predictable formula for the growth of the prison/industrial complex, I can't imagine what it would be.

The Republican-dominated Congress is hostile to the SNAP program (fueled by the false Reagan-era narrative of brown "welfare queens," since they seem to be perpetually stuck in the Reagan era) and cuts the very programs that many of their own Republican voters badly need. That's what you call hitting at the wrong target! The reality is that there is such commonality among the challenging circumstances facing many US citizens, irrespective of ethnicity, that it is almost impossible to target just one group of people with precision without having many unintended casualties as well. A prominent exception would be the differentiation in criminal penalties between powdered cocaine and crystalline cocaine (crack).

These unintended victims of bad legislation are "represented" by members of Congress who serve in uncompetitive, gerrymandered districts and can enact policies contrary to the best interests of their own constituents and *still* get reelected. Why? Because the false narrative or belief—the okeydoke—that the "fiscally responsible" (conservative) Republicans are reducing benefits to keep the brown "welfare cheats" in line, even if their own voters are injured in the process.

That's somewhat similar to the recent proliferation of voter-ID bills designed to combat voter fraud, which is almost nonexistent. An August 6, 2014, *Washington Post* article submitted by Justin Levitt said "A comprehensive investigation of voter impersonation finds thirty-one credible incidents out of one billion ballots cast." The numbers didn't lie. It is a "solution" desperately

Because there were thirty-one verifiable instances, across the nation, of voter impersonation *that's .000000031 percent from over a billion ballots cast in this country between 2000 and 2014.*

searching for a problem. Punishing and hindering citizens with the legitimate right and privilege to vote and justifying it because there were thirty-one verifiable instances, across the nation, of voter impersonation is criminal. For the math wonks out there, *that's .000000031 percent from over a billion ballots cast in this country between 2000 and 2014.* Passing voter-ID laws does not address the more likely but still rare voting fraud schemes, such as absentee-ballot abuse or registering to vote in more than one place. It is a solution in search of a problem. It is bad policy. Worse (but intended) results occur as seniors, poor people, brown people, and young people are the *legal* voters who are most negatively affected by this election law, "ballot security" scam.

I have always been much more concerned about *real* ballot security that addresses computerized voting machines *with no paper trail* than I ever was about voter impersonation at the polls. It is much easier to steal an election using a rogue computer algorithm in a computerized voting machine than to arrange teams of voter impersonators to descend upon polling places. What are the political leanings of the companies that produce the paperless voting machines? *That* concerns me!

An article in the *Free Press* on March 20, 2004, entitled "Voting Paper Trail Advocate Dies in 'Tragic Accident'" recounted the untimely and suspicious death of Athan Gibbs, who was a tireless advocate for developing voting machines that truly provided a paper trail that could help to prevent a repeat of the 2000 election debacle.

"The subject line on Tuesday's email read: 'Another mysterious accident … Athan Gibbs dead, Diebold lives.'"

The story that followed addressed the sudden, tragic, and untimely death of perhaps the nation's most insistent advocate for a verifiable voting machine paper trail in place of the ubiquitous touchscreen voting systems.

Gibbs was an accountant with more than thirty years' experience who felt compelled to design the TruVote system in the wake of the 2000 Florida presidential election debacle. He was killed on Friday, March 12, 2004, when his car collided with an eighteen-wheeler.

Some will insist that Gibbs's death was simply an unfortunate coincidence. However, the article observes:

Gibbs' death bears heightened scrutiny because of the way he lived his life" after the 2000 presidential election. "I interviewed Athan Gibbs in January of this year." He said, "I've been an accountant, an auditor, for more than thirty years. Electronic voting machines that don't supply a paper trail go against every principle of accounting and auditing that's being taught in American business schools.

The machines typically used by American businesses for the purposes of tabulation and auditing are designed to provide paper trails. Gibbs asserted that there isn't a business in America that would purchase or use a machine that didn't produce a paper trail to verify transaction results. How much more concerning is it that our country uses voting machines that, according to experts, can be easily hacked and have no paper trail?

The way Gibbs's TruVote machine works is this: after the voter touches the screen to make their choices, a paper ballot prints out. The voter can then compare what appears on paper with the votes they intended to cast. Once they have confirmed the accuracy of the printed ballot, the ballot is then dropped into a lockbox, and the voter receives a numbered receipt. The receipt allows the voter to track their ballot to ensure that it was transported to the central location for the tabulation of votes. The paper ballot is also a reliable backup to the votes electronically registered in the machine so in the event of a recount, the paper ballots can *accurately* determine the will of the voters. *What a concept!*

If elected officials were *truly* interested in ensuring that voting results accurately reflected the will of the voters, they would insist that voting technology similar to the TruVote system was used throughout the country. Instead, their voter ID laws merely attempt to shrink the electorate to give the proclaimers of the legislators' particular political ideology a greater chance of winning, even though their policies have not been favorably received by a majority of American citizens. I wish I could say this was curious, but it's incredibly obvious and has been hidden in plain sight, with no apologies.

In the December 2013, *National Review* article "Appalachia: The Big White Ghetto," author Kevin Williamson wrote:

> Appalachian towns and villages stretching from northern Mississippi to southern New York, [are] a slowly dissipating nebula of poverty and misery with its heart in eastern Kentucky, the last redoubt of the Scots-Irish working class that picked up where African slave labor left off, mining and cropping and sawing the raw materials for a modern American economy that would soon run out of profitable uses for the class of people who 500 years ago would have been known, without any derogation, as peasants.

[This is Classism 101: Y'all would have been considered peasants five hundred years ago—and you *still* are now!]

There is not much focus on the future in these parts. The future seems bleak and persistently unchanging. As a result, there is a reliance upon pills and dope and beer first thing in the morning, just to make it through yet another mind-numbing, soul-crushing day. The recipients of public assistance, which is widespread, "trade cases of food-stamp Pepsi for packs of Kentucky's Best cigarettes" and cash and "the occasional blast of meth." Their lives are filled with meetings of Narcotics Anonymous, petty crime, and "the recreational making and surgical unmaking of teenaged mothers." Life expectancies are short; the average man here dies more than a decade earlier than a man in Fairfax County, Virginia. Women's life expectancy has declined, as well, by 1.1 percent between 1987 and 2007.

If the people here weren't 98.5 percent white, we'd call it a reservation.

> Like its black urban counterparts, the Big White Ghetto suffers from a whole trainload of social problems, but the most significant among them may be adverse selection. The people who have the necessary work skills, "the academic ability, or the

simple desperate native enterprising grit to do so get the hell out as fast as they can, and they have been doing that for decades.

For those left behind, the business community continues to weaken, the institutions and social networks upon which they used to rely have eroded, and there is no real reason for those who remain to have any hope. As a result, there is a heightened level of both drug addiction and welfare fraud. Nevertheless, the crime rate throughout Appalachia is only about two-thirds of the national average. Perhaps that can be attributed to the fact that in spite of all that ails them, these communities are still, largely, family enclaves where most of the folks are kin or know one another at the very least.

The similarities between urban ghettos and Appalachian white ghettos are eerie and unsettling. Yet should it really surprise us? Poverty is poverty, no matter how you color it. The real shame is that all of these impoverished people have been convinced that the other is their enemy, and that as long as they are not the other, they have someone to look down on. This false sense of self-delusional pyrrhic comfort stands as a huge barrier to people in similar circumstances with similar challenges, who should instead band together to insist upon comprehensive, systemic change for *all* who are oppressed and marginalized.

Chapter 4

HIDDEN IN PLAIN SIGHT

Rich people have always stayed on top, by dividing
white people from colored people. But white people
got more in common with colored people than
they do with rich people.
— *Senator Jay Billington Bulworth*

I am a movie lover. There's nothing I enjoy more than a good
movie, whatever the genre, although I often lean toward science
fiction. For the portion of the viewing audience that is willing
to perceive it, there are kernels of truth about the lie of race or the
corrupt system of government and finance in entertainment.

In episode 70 of the original *Star Trek* series, entitled "Let
That Be Your Last Battlefield," the *Enterprise* takes on a passenger
seeking asylum. A cop from the same planet tracks him down to
the *Enterprise* and ultimately takes over the ship. Each man shares
the distinction of being white on one half of his body and black
(*actually* black, not just brown) on the other. The planet they have
left is engaged in a war between these two races. When someone
observes that the two look the same, the cop's indignant response is,
"Are you blind? I'm white on the right side!" The episode, conceived
by Gene Rodenberry and his creative team, was intended to speak
to a world in the late 1960s that was in the throes of the civil rights
movement and was fixated on matters of race. This episode intended
to display the absurdity of our concept and understanding of race.

The two antagonists were locked in a literal life-or-death struggle over differences that were *truly* only skin deep. Sound familiar? In the final scene of the story, the aliens have commandeered the *Enterprise* to return to their home planet so the fugitive can receive justice for his crime—the crime of encouraging rebellion because he and his people wanted to be treated as equals. When the two transport themselves back to the surface, all that is left of the planet is flames and smoldering embers. Yet these last two combatants, the last living persons from a planet which has literally fought to the death over differences that were only skin deep, resume their fight with one another, among the flames and the embers—to the death.

In our society, and on this planet, where we face any number of real threats and concerns, will we ever focus our energies on those concerns that really matter? Or are we fated to simply fight the old familiar and misguided fight—to the death? As stated before, "When you know better, you have to do better." If not, that which is only skin deep may become our last battlefield—an utter and complete waste of energy, time, resources, and lives!

I also recommend the 1995 film *White Man's Burden*, starring John Travolta and Harry Belafonte. In this cinematic experience that takes place in an alternative America, blacks are members of the economic and social elite, and whites are inhabitants of inner-city ghettos. There is a Sioux prayer that says, "Oh Great Spirit, keep me from ever judging a man until I have walked a mile in his moccasins." For an hour and a half, the movie invites us to put the shoe on the other foot to get a glimpse into how the other half lives.

> There is a Sioux prayer that says, "Oh Great Spirit, keep me from ever judging a man until I have walked a mile in his moccasins."

The significant, systemic injustices Travolta's character, Louis Pinnock, has to face just for being a minority (white) in a society that favors blacks are both instructive and enraging. As we are granted a bird's-eye view into the life of each main character, we are treated to the litany of slights and struggles faced by Pinnock and his family. We also experience the racist assumptions and the self-absorbed paternalism exhibited by the black people as they deign to bestow charity on the poor white kids, who are herded onto the stage at a charity event like a litter of lost puppies.

Pinnock is a struggling factory worker doing the best he can to support his wife and two children. Belafonte, as Thaddeus Thomas, is the factory owner. Pinnock accepts a request from his supervisor to deliver something to Thomas's house. He is uncertain of which entrance to use and inadvertently catches a glimpse of Mrs. Thomas wrapped in a towel. Mr. Thomas, confusing the white man as a Peeping Tom, shares his fury with Pinnock's supervisor, and this costs Pinnock his job. Pinnock goes back to Thomas's house to try to speak with Thaddeus but can never make it past the gate. Then comes the downward spiral where the falsely accused Pinnock is unable to find other work, in spite of repeated trips to the employment agency. He has a bad run-in with the police (black cops, of course) where he allegedly fits the description and gets rousted and then abused by the arrogant and overzealous cops. Things get even worse when, the next morning, his landlord shows up with the sheriff to evict Pinnock and his family. Simmering barely beneath the surface are consistent tensions between Pinnock and his wife, often witnessed by their young son, over their challenged finances. Adding to the discord is the low regard in which he is vocally and derisively held by his mother-in-law.

Desiring to clear his name, Pinnock returns to Thomas's house, kidnaps him, and demands (just) $3,000, which were his lost wages, so he can secure a place for his family to live and to be able to pay his bills. Afterward is a series of unfortunate events that ultimately result in the Pinnock further enduring the unabated plight of the poor, while the rich man returns to his position of power and influence.

While the plot might seem heavy-handed or implausible to some, it feels maddeningly familiar to African Americans who have to deal with these types of slights and abuses on an almost daily basis. As NAACP chairperson Roslyn Brock stated in her remarks at the 2016 National Convention, "Being black in America is exhausting!" Yet, unless one has dared to try to walk in the "moccasins" of another, to get a glimpse of their reality, one will remain comfortably, blissfully, and persistently ignorant about the struggles of the other. As Thaddeus does at one point in the movie, one might also disdainfully blame the victim for his own life circumstances and the choices that ensue from those circumstances. The movie made me both angry and sad as the story careened toward its seemingly inevitable conclusion, with the poor man dead, while life went on for everyone else—aside from Pinnock's own family, of course.

White Man's Burden cinematically poses the question educator Jane Elliott, the originator of the "Blue Eyes-Brown Eyes" experiment, asked a majority white audience:

> "I want every white person in this room who would be happy to be treated as this society in general treats our black citizens … if you as a white person would be happy to receive the same treatment that our black citizens do in this society, please stand." She then repeats the question. "You didn't understand the directions … if you white folks want to be treated the way blacks are in this society, stand … Nobody is standing here. That says very plainly that you know what's happening; you know you don't want it for you. I want to know why you are so willing to accept it or to allow it to happen for others?"

In one of her appearances on *The Oprah Winfrey Show*, Elliott quoted a thirty-year-old document that asserts that racism is mental illness. "Racism was defined by the President's Joint Council on Mental Health in Children in 1959 as being 'the number one mental health problem among children in the United States.' Racism is learned behavior … it is taught." Even in the

> "**R**acism was defined by the President's Joint Council on Mental Health in Children in 1959 as being 'the number one mental health problem among children in the United States.'

twenty-first century, where we have the technological resources to conclusively separate fact from fiction and scientifically verifiable realities from cultural and historical lore, we continue to choose the familiar narrative over the accurate one. *Insanity* has been defined as "doing the same thing over and over again, expecting different results." (Just sayin'.)

In addition to matters of ethnic hostility, cinema will occasionally deal in some truth about income inequality and the rigged game (aka the okeydoke) in which we are forced to live. In the movie *In Time*, the coin of the realm was *literally* time. Any purchase one wanted to make for food, housing, or anything else was made in minutes, hours, days, and years—in time. Everyone would live until the age of twenty-five off the clock. At that point, a clock located on their forearm would begin to count down the hours, minutes, and seconds of the final year of their lives. There were only two ways to get more time: be born into wealth, so it was not a concern to you, or to work in a factory, producing riches for the wealthy but barely earning enough to stay alive from one pay period to the next. Time could be transferred from one person to the next by having a time meter dispense time into their forearm or by clasping forearms, but if they could not reach a person willing to give them some time—in time—they would die on the spot and could not be revived.

After the death of his mother, who was literally running down the street trying to get to her son in time, Will Salas, played by Justin Timberlake, encounters and helps a wealthy man who is clearly on the wrong side of town and in danger of being robbed or killed. At the age of 105 (but still appearing 25) he is tired of living a self-centered, pointless, and seemingly endless existence. He chooses to "clock out" (to die), but he dispenses all of his time, but a few minutes, to Will while he is asleep. After the man dies, Will is able to use the time gifted to him and is able to access the world of the wealthy. When the time cops find the dead wealthy man's body, they assume wrongdoing and begin a frantic search to find the culprit. In spite of the fact that they have enough evidence to prove Will did *not* commit any crime, they basically assert that he is not worthy to have that time. They take most of the time away from him. This leads to several chase scenes, and include an attempt by Will and

Sylvia Weis, played by Amanda Seyfried, the daughter of one of the world's wealthiest people, to stop playing by the rules and to rob time banks and dispense the time to other poor people. They also encounter some of the criminal element who abuse the poor and the struggling with the full knowledge of the police.

The most hidden-in-plain-sight truism of this movie, for me, comes after Will and Sylvia have robbed a local bank and shared the time with poor people in the community. Rather than allowing poor people to have more buying power, *those in control of prices simply raise the prices in the community, so that the new additional time they have will buy less.* Ever wonder how even though you can be making more money, you can never get caught up, let alone get ahead? Think about how much things—a loaf of bread, a gallon of milk, a gallon of gas, school tuition, a house—*used* to cost when you were younger. The more we earn, the more things cost. We are paddling faster and faster, but it still feels as if we're more or less in the same place, in the same financial condition we were in before. These are the burdens and indignities that classism heaps upon all of us, irrespective of ethnicity or color. Our obsession with things that are of middling or no real importance keep us from focusing on what is really being done to us. Then the irrational focus on skin color—which is tantamount to less than one-tenth of 1 percent of our total genetic composition—keeps us strategically separated from persons of similar condition and in similar need. Just keep blaming brown people for everything, and let the real culprits, the greedy wealthy, off the hook.

> The irrational focus on skin color—which is tantamount to less than one-tenth of 1 percent of our total genetic composition—keeps us strategically separated from persons of similar condition and in similar need.

In the movie, during a moment in between chase scenes, Will asks Sylvia, "How can you live with yourself watching people die right next to you?"

She replies, without a hint of irony or malice, "You don't watch. You close your eyes."

People who were considered wealthy had access to enough time to remain young almost indefinitely. They lived in an isolated area—what one might call the ultimate gated community—entirely separated from the people whose labor made their luxuries possible, and who had to scrape for every minute and every hour of their lives.

The fact that my time is dispensed through a *garden hose* rather than with a thimble makes me feel good about myself: "I've arrived!" That is, until I see that the time of some others is dispensed to them by a *fire hose*! Is there anything intrinsically better about one person than another? Absolutely not! Imagine the caste system among the Hindus in India, in which one's place in society is determined entirely by the circumstances of one's birth. What a waste of human potential to consign a large segment of the population to poverty and "Untouchable" status for life, because of who their parents are! I understand that this system is tied into their spiritual belief in reincarnation, and they believe that people can be born into a better stratum in their next lives. However, since this is the only life we can be *sure* we're going to have, to willingly accept the suffering of large groups of our fellow human beings strikes me as cruel.

A final observation about the movie is the obsessive and frantic pursuit of Will by the time cop Raymond Leon, played by Cillian Murphy. In one of the most telling quotes in the movie, he says, "If you put enough time in the 'wrong hands' [quotation marks added], you upset the whole system. His crime wasn't taking time; he's giving it away." Had Will been willing to become greedy, wealthy, self-indulgent, keep a low profile, and keep his time for himself, he might have been able to live a quiet life of pampered luxury. Instead he chose to share the time with as many people as possible—mostly people he did not know.

Who among us is willing to share what we cannot keep, in order to gain what we cannot lose? If the 95 percent get sick and tired of being sick and tired and insist on comprehensive, systemic changes, there's nothing anyone else can really do about it except to get with our program—those things that meet the needs and demands of the larger population. (In the next chapter, a reference to the protests in France a few years back speak to this dynamic.)

The most in-your-face treatment of the okeydoke, in my opinion, is the 1998 movie *Bulworth*, starring and produced by Warren Beatty as California US Senator Jay Billington Bulworth, who is in a campaign for reelection. After Bulworth takes out a contract to have himself killed so his daughter can be the beneficiary of his $10 million insurance policy, he is then strangely liberated to speak his mind without filters on the issues of the day and the realities of politics (both his and others'). He speaks with a reckless candor about who gets served by elected officials, who does not, and why. In all of the succeeding campaign appearances, Bulworth is brutally honest. When speaking to a room full of wealthy donors, he speaks about the need to raise $10,000 a day toward his next campaign, explaining why he and others feel it is necessary to suck up to them and to advocate policies the donors like, even if they're bad for the country as a whole, just so they can be reelected. In the same way, he speaks at an African American church and actually tells the people the truth—that their issues and concerns are and will remain unresponded to [malicious neglect] because they make no campaign contributions. In essence, they can't afford to pay to play.

During his walk on the liberated side, Bulworth encounters constituents he would never meet in his normal itinerary and hears their assessment about their conditions and the impoverished neighborhoods in which they live, the poor schools their children attend, and all manner of social commentary. Further liberated by alcohol and some weed, Bulworth appears on TV for a campaign interview, clad like he's "from the 'hood." In a sometimes-profane rant that is occasionally presented in a rap-style cadence, he regurgitates what he has heard from community members earlier. One of the most meaningful

Rich people have *always* stayed on top, by dividing white people from colored people. But white people got more in common with colored people than they do with rich people."

and true statements he makes is that "We got Americans with families can't even buy a meal. Ask a brother whose been downsized if he's getting any deal. Or a white boy busting ass till they put him in his grave. You ain't gotta be a black boy to be living like a slave. Rich people have *always* stayed on top, by dividing white people from colored people. But white people got more in common with colored people than they do with rich people."

The controversial film had a limited release, but was critically acclaimed and was nominated for numerous awards including Best Original Screenplay for the Seventy-First Academy Awards and Best Picture for the Fifty-Sixth Golden Globes. It won Best Screenplay from the Los Angeles Film Critics Association. This movie spoke with brutal and humorous candor about the state of our republic and the sorry, sold-out, and self-absorbed condition of our BS politics— another example of brutal truths and realities that are hidden in plain sight.

Finally, 2016's *Free State of Jones* recounts historical events that took place during and after the Civil War. Matthew McConaughey plays the role of Newt Knight, a poor Mississippi farmer who was a battlefield nurse in the Confederate Army. He got to see the suffering and mayhem of war up close. He becomes further disillusioned when he learns that the oldest son coming from a family that owns at least twenty slaves was exempted from military service and could return home. If the family owed forty slaves or more, the second son could go home, and so on, in increments of twenty. After his fourteen-year-old nephew is conscripted and killed almost as soon as he gets to the battlefield, Newt decides to take his body back home so his mother can bury him. Once there, he decides not to return to the war, marking him as a deserter.

Now at home, he begins to see how the forces of the wealthy and the military are pillaging the rest of his friends and family in Jones County, Mississippi. Families are expected to give 10 percent of their produce to the war effort. Instead, the military stops by their farms whenever they choose and takes almost 90 percent, rather than the 10 percent they said they would. All of these experiences bring the reality of true "class warfare," by which I mean warfare waged for the benefit of the wealthy economic class, with poor folks as the pawns. [In the game of chess, the pawns, the *least*-valuable pieces, are usually sacrificed first.] He sees the conflict *"as a rich man's war and a poor man's fight."* Newt begins to lead a rebellion in response to the forced conscription of young men and the decimation of the food and livestock of the poor farmers.

Shortly thereafter, he flees the authorities and ends up taking refuge in the swamps with runaway slaves. After a while, more deserters end up taking refuge in the swamps too. They begin to form a community where these poor farmers and ex-slaves must depend upon one another to survive. There was certainly no racial kumbaya moment in their community; the long-stoked and intentionally manipulated contention between brown and white reared its ugly head from time to time. But at a key moment, when everyone was hiding out in the swamp, one of the poor white farmers told one of the "niggers" that he wasn't entitled to the food the whites were eating. (These were the same "niggers" who had shown the poor white folks and deserters how to find the swamp hideaway in the first place!) In the cinematic telling of the story, Newt points out to his fellow white swamp dweller that "we're all niggers." In the context of being people who were on the run and considered contraband and criminals, he explained, they were all the same and had a common foe. They were all poor people fighting for their freedom and independence from having to support the lifestyle of the plantation gentry class with their blood, sweat, and even their very lives.

When they formally declared themselves the "Free State of Jones," there were four guiding principles:

1) "No man ought to stay poor so another man can get rich." The purpose for one man (or woman) to exist should not be to make and keep another person rich. If that were the case, what an utterly frustrating and meaningless existence that would be—to live solely to benefit and profit someone else.

2) "No man ought to tell another man what he's got to live for or what he's got to die for." That lines up with what Newt said earlier, that the war was "a rich man's war and a poor man's fight." [That dynamic still exists with today's all-volunteer military. Many of our troops come from communities where

the prospects for their lives and the ability to support their families is bleak. So they choose to enlist in the military as a way to support their families and improve their lot in life. Of course, since the military is all volunteer, that means that these sons and daughters from economically challenged communities—the other 1 percent who serve our country in the armed forces—can be kept in a state of war for over a decade (the longest continuous period in American history) while the children of wealth and privilege don't have the slightest worry of ever being called upon to serve. If we still had the draft in the United States, we absolutely would not have invaded a country that didn't attack us (Iraq), and we absolutely would not have been in a constant state of war for the past thirteen years!]

3) "What you put in the ground is yours to tend and harvest, and no man ought to be able to take that away from you." No one has the right to come into the community to tax or commandeer the livestock or produce you need to feed your family and survive.

4) "Every man's a man. If you can walk on two legs, you're a man. It's as simple as that." We are all men, God's children of sacred worth and valued, equally, in the sight of God.

The great value of this movie, in my estimation, is that it brings into sharp relief the fact that there was common cause between poor whites and the formerly enslaved against the moneyed interests that were pimping them all. Brown people, who were not even considered human, were brutalized and denied the fruits of their labor. Poor white people who were barely landowners were made to feel better about their sorry lot in that, at least, they weren't Negroes. Nevertheless, they too were pimped by the plantation owners and moneyed interests. They were conscripted to fight and die in the "rich man's war," while their families were left struggling in their absence. In this (and many other) instances, it truly seems that the more things change, the more they remain the same. Today, members of Congress blather on and on about "supporting our troops" while the mics and cameras are on but then cut entitlements and benefits that our warriors have earned, when they feel no one is looking. It is sad that in this century, there are still family members of our soldiers, sailors, airmen, and marines who must seek public assistance to make ends meet while their poor sons, daughters, husbands, and wives continue to fight rich men's wars ad infinitum.

Chapter 5

THE OKEYDOKE— LET THE GAMES BEGIN

If you can convince the lowest white man he's better than the best colored man, he won't know you're picking his pocket. Hell, give him someone to look down on, and he'll empty his pockets for you.
— *President Lyndon Baines Johnson*

As stated in the introduction, I have found the book *A People's History of the United States* written by Professor Howard Zinn to be instructive in helping us better understand how we got where we are in this country. Further, we also need to grasp the demonstrable fact that it has *not* happened by accident or as a result of any inherent malice or natural disconnect between people of different ethnicities. It is intentional, by design, with premeditated malice, and for the purpose of keeping people with like interests separated over skin-deep nonsense. In this chapter, I will quote liberally from *A People's History*, with comment, to use Zinn's considerable scholarship and research to lay out the case concerning the malicious intentionality of the manipulated disconnect between one expression of the human family from another and how these lies are taking us on a path to ruin.

In the second chapter of *A People's History*, "Drawing the Color Line," W. E. B. DuBois talked about the problem of the "color line."

At the time of the writing of Zinn's masterpiece, and even today, this was and is a problem that we still face. It is not a rhetorical question; in order to truly understand where we are now, however, we must first understand, how it began. DuBois asked, "Is it possible for whites and blacks to live together without hatred?" In order for that to happen, we must intentionally unlearn many of the false and malicious things we were told about one another and about ourselves. We must begin with the truism that "none of us is inherently better than anyone else" and then build from there.

One of the counterpoints frequently made about slavery in the United States is that slavery was not a new phenomenon in the world. There is also truth to the claim that some Africans facilitated the stealing of other Africans, in exchange for material gain, for the purpose of enslavement on these shores. Indeed, the trans-Atlantic slave trade could not have been conducted on as large a scale without the complicit cooperation of other Africans.

Yet Zinn notes:

> African slavery is hardly to be praised. But it was far different from plantation or mining slavery in the Americas, which was lifelong, morally crippling, destructive of family ties, without hope of any future. African slavery lacked two elements that made American slavery the most cruel form of slavery in history: the frenzy for limitless profit that comes from capitalistic agriculture; the reduction of the slave to less than human status by the use of racial hatred, with that relentless clarity based on color, where white was master, black was slave.[1]

According to the Trans-Atlantic Slave Trade Database, between 1525 and 1866, in the entire history of the slave trade to the New World, *12.5 million Africans* were shipped to the New World. Some *10.7 million* survived the dreaded Middle Passage, disembarking in North America, the Caribbean, and South America. Zinn estimates that Africa lost as many as fifty million human beings to slavery and death, to serve as the free labor to build modern Western civilization. It was upon the backs of these millions of stolen and enslaved Africans that the "modern Western civilization" in the future United States was built.

This enslavement was not easily accepted by the stolen Africans. There were many instances when they escaped from their enslavement. Gerald Mullin, in his work, *Flight and Rebellion,* found ads in newspapers, placed between 1736 and 1801, for over a thousand men and women who had escaped their bondage. The most compelling reason for the enslaved to risk maiming and death, if recaptured, was to find members of their family who had been sold away. Part of the insidious "logic" of slavery in North America was to destroy families and weaken the resolve of the enslaved by forbidding marriage and breaking up families.

In spite of the malicious and hideous culture of American chattel slavery, there was a deep and abiding desire among the stolen Africans to remain connected with their loved ones. They would risk death and dismemberment to find their family members once they had been sold off.

As the intentionally pernicious system of slavery developed, slave owners sought to instill as much control over their slaves as possible. They were indoctrinated to believe that their brown skin was a symbol for their "divine" designation to a role and lifetime of service. They were even indoctrinated to believe that the lighter brown a person was, the more preferred treatment they deserved and would receive. There is no doubt that more favorable treatment was due, in part, to the fact that many were a part of the slave owner's *own* bloodline, due to his unwelcome nocturnal visits to the slave quarters.

The abuse endured by the enslaved Africans was not only physical but also psychological. They withstood many beatings. As the skin tone of some of the enslaved began to lighten, as a result of the aforementioned nocturnal visits (aka rape), a stratification of treatment and status was used to divide the enslaved. Those with lighter skin tone received more preferential treatment. The seeds for dissension between the "house niggers" and the "field niggers" had been sown. Zinn also referred to the "lulling effects of religion" that also undermined the sense of self-worth and value of the enslaved. The pernicious logic was to tell the stolen Africans that even God held them in lesser regard and had assigned them to a role of permanent servitude, obeisance, and inferiority.

On the subject of the "lulling effects of religion," I remember reading the autobiography of Reverend Dr. Howard Thurman. He spoke of reading the Bible to his grandmother, who was formerly enslaved. He noted that she didn't want to hear anything from the apostle Paul, except for First Corinthians 13, the "love chapter." That was because the only texts the "authorized" preachers would use when they preached on slave plantations were the texts stating "slaves be obedient to your masters." Even though she was an illiterate slave, Thurman's grandmother instinctively knew there was more to her God than that the handful of repetitive readings she was allowed to hear. Nevertheless, this illustration cites the strategic and calculated way in which slave owners even tried to control the stolen Africans' spiritual lives.

The Misuse of the Bible to Justify Racism and Prejudice

While on the topic of the Bible, I want to take a quick break from Zinn to address some of the biblical misinterpretations/lies that have been used as rationale for apartheid, Jim Crow, and all kinds of racial lies that have been perpetrated in the name of religion and in the name of God.

One of the advantages of having a historical record in writing is that once it has been written/recorded, one need not parse or debate what the person actually said or meant; they said it themselves. Again, the Bible has often been used to justify racial prejudice, white supremacy (the ideology that whites are *the* superior representation of the *Homo sapiens* created order all around the world). William T. Thompson, the cofounder of the *Savannah Morning News* (formerly known as the *Daily Morning News*) has incorrectly been credited with designing the Confederate flag (the "Stars and Bars") in the 1850s. It was first used in the First Battle of Manassas in 1861 and was designed by Confederate Generals Beauregard, Johnston and Cabell. It did become the Confederate national flag in 1863. In an editorial about that flag, written April 28, 1863, William T. Thompson wrote the following:

> As a people, we are fighting to maintain the *Heaven-ordained* [emphasis mine] supremacy of the White man over the inferior or colored race. As a national emblem, it (the confederate flag) is significant of our higher cause, the cause of a superior race ... such a flag ... would soon take the rank among the proudest ensigns of the nations and be hailed by the civilized world as THE WHITE MAN'S FLAG. [I suppose that is why the modern-day Nazis in Europe often fly this "White man's flag," since the Nazi swastika flag has been banned.]

Reading what Thompson wrote, and given the fact that he even deigned to attribute to "heaven" (God) the "supremacy" of the white man, I would submit that the Confederate flag is hardly the benign symbol of cultural heritage or regional pride it has been made out to be.

Further, before the Civil War, the vice president of the confederacy, Alexander H. Stephens, said in an 1861 speech in South Carolina that the Confederacy was not founded on the "false idea" that all men are created equal. "The Confederacy, by contrast, is founded upon exactly the opposite idea; its foundations are laid, its cornerstone rests, upon the great truth that the Negro is not equal to the white man; that slavery, subordination to the superior race, is his natural and moral condition." More than one million people were killed or wounded during this War Between the States, founded upon the false notion, which misappropriated, misquoted, and misinterpreted scripture to support the lie, that one ethnic group (race) is inherently superior to another.

Over the years, many a lie and numerous ideologies have been based upon these lies on the Bible! It should be noted (and may come as a surprise to some) that most of the activity in the Bible did *not* occur in Europe. The biblical story begins in Africa and was ultimately exported from there to the rest of the world. At the very beginning of the Bible in Genesis, chapter 2, the rivers flowing through the garden of Eden are the Pishon, the Gihon (which "winds through the entire land of Cush," the region south of Egypt, including the parts of the present countries of Ethiopia and Sudan), the Tigris, and the Euphrates. The Pihon and the Gihon are also known as the Blue and White Nile River, respectively. Where is the Nile? Africa! "Why is that pertinent?" you ask. Because *in the context of the lies told to and about the stolen*

> **I**t should be noted that most of the activity in the Bible did *not* occur in Europe. The biblical story begins in Africa and was ultimately exported from there to the rest of the world.

Africans and the abuses heaped upon their descendants, it is crucial to acknowledge that when using the Bible as a source book, the biblical story has its origin in Africa, and a majority of it takes place there. The lie told to brown people that "Christianity is the white man's religion" couldn't be further from the truth. Africans are at center stage, along with other members of the human family, throughout the "holy writ."

The first lie told is when Cain killed his brother, Abel was turned black by God as a mark of punishment. But, *hidden in plain sight*, in the actual words written in the Bible, Genesis chapter 4, verse 15 states, *"The Lord put a mark on Cain so that no one who found him would kill him."* My friends, it was a mark of protection, *not* a mark of cursing. If it was blackness *and* a mark of protection, then most black people are surely waiting for that protection to kick in!

The next lie has to do with the wholly made-up "curse of Ham." Again, the truth is *hidden in plain sight*, right in the text! In Genesis 9:21–27, Noah becomes intoxicated, ends up naked, and then passes out. Ham sees his father's nakedness (looks upon it—some interpretations even imply that he laughed) and tells his brothers Shem and Japheth. Those two then walk into their father's tent backward, so as not to see his nakedness, and they cover him up. When Noah awakens and finds out what happened, he pronounces a curse on Canaan, one of Ham's sons. So there is *no* curse of Hamitic peoples (thought to be the foreparents of brown people in the world) because it was Ham's *son*, Canaan, who was cursed. Further, it was *not* a curse pronounced by God, but rather by an angry father/grandfather with a hangover. Nevertheless, these have been two of the key biblical rationalizations to justify racism and the inhuman treatment visited upon brown people.

The third rationale is based on the Lord telling His people of Israel not to intermingle with the surrounding nations and not to give their daughters or sons in marriage, etc. This is not based on anything race as much as it is God's desire for His people to remain separate from the heathen religious practices of the surrounding nations. The intention was to prevent them from diverting their attention away from the Lord to the idolatrous religious practices of others. Again, there is no "racial" component here, but religious/spiritual.

Finally, there is the whole misbelief that the artistic renderings of Jesus from the Renaissance period are an *actual* representation of the biblical, historic Jesus. First, a question from Jesus' early life: Who would send a lily-white, blond-haired Jesus with his white parents to hide from Herod in black Egypt? They would stick out like a sore thumb. (Doesn't really seem like a real discreet plan to me. "We're looking for a white couple with a white baby. Anybody seen them?") The description of Jesus in Revelation 1:14–15 is also instructive. "His head and hair were white like *wool*, as white as snow, and his eyes were blazing like fire. His feet were like *bronze* glowing in a furnace." I can't imagine why Jesus would need to change from being a white guy in life to being a brown guy in his resurrected form.

Why take this much time to address biblical racism?

(1) In spite of the fact that there are numerous folks who do not believe in the Bible, there are billions of people around the world who do. To the extent that any of them still try to justify their prejudices today based on the Bible, it needed to be addressed.

(2) The Bible is the story of *all* of God's creation, not just one ethnic group with all the others intended to bow down before that group. As it says in Romans 2:11, "God does not show favoritism

(partiality)." "God is no respecter of persons" (Acts 10:34), and "there is neither Jew nor Greek, slave nor free, male nor female, for you are all one in Christ Jesus" (Galatians 3:28).

[*That* is a verse Howard Thurman's grandmother almost surely did *not* hear while she was enslaved!] We are *all* "fearfully and wonderfully made" (Psalm 139:14). We are *all* made in God's image and likeness (Genesis 1:27). My God is not one who fosters, foments, or encourages racial animus or superiority by any of His creation toward any others among His creation! Does God prefer your skin color or mine? We all come from the same dirt.

> **D**oes God prefer your skin color or mine? We all come from the same dirt.

It's All about Control

After intentionally maiming the self-worth of the stolen Africans and depriving them of their family, their language, and their culture, the greatest challenge was to maintain control over them *and* the indentured white servants who labored alongside them. They were in the same disadvantaged position and found in one another allies of common circumstance. Zinn writes:

> From time to time, whites were involved in the slave resistance. As early as 1663, indentured white servants and black slaves in Gloucester County, Virginia, formed a conspiracy to rebel and gain their freedom. The plot was betrayed, and ended with executions. (Gerald) Mullin reports (*Flight and Rebellion* studying 18th century slave resistance) that the newspaper notices of runaways in Virginia often warned "ill-disposed" whites about harboring fugitives. Sometimes slaves and free men ran off together, or cooperated in crimes together.[2]

As (Edmund) Morgan writes, masters, "initially at least, perceived slaves in much the same way they had always perceived servants ... shiftless, irresponsible, unfaithful, ungrateful, dishonest." And "if freemen with disappointed hopes should make common cause with slaves of desperate hope, the results might be worse than anything Bacon had done" ... And so, measures were taken. "About the same time that slave codes involving discipline and punishment, were passed by the Virginia assembly, Virginia's ruling class, having proclaimed that all white men were superior to black, went on to offer their social (but white) inferiors a number of benefits previously denied them. In 1705, a law was passed requiring masters to provide white servants whose indenture time was up with 10 bushels of corn, 30 shillings, and a gun, while women servants were to get 15 bushels of corn and 40 shillings. Also, the newly freed servants were to get 50 acres of land.[3]

Morgan concludes, "... once the small planter felt less exploited by taxation and began to prosper a little, he became less turbulent, less dangerous, more respectable. He could begin to see his big neighbor not as an extortionist but is a powerful protector of their common interests."

We see now a complex web of historical threads to ensnare blacks for slavery in America: the desperation of starving settlers, the special helplessness of the displaced African, the powerful incentive of profit for slave trader and planter, the temptation of superior status for poor whites, the elaborate controls against escape and rebellion, the legal and social punishment of black and white collaboration.

The point is that the elements of this web are historical, not "natural." This does not mean that they are easily disentangled or dismantled. It means only that there is a possibility for something else, under historical conditions not yet realized. *And one of these conditions would be the elimination of that class exploitation which has made poor whites desperate for small gifts of status, and has prevented that unity of black and white necessary for joint rebellion and reconstruction.*[4]

The common bond white and brown servants felt was intentionally and strategically undermined by granting the white indentured servants the *slightest* advantage over the enslaved Africans. Their white skin separated them from and made them better than the enslaved Africans who were in almost the same conditions. While the Africans were enslaved *for life* (with few having the opportunity to secure their freedom), whites served out their time of indenture and then were granted money, a gun, and land as a parting gift. *The great demarcation between brown and white had begun.*

In chapter 3, "Persons of Mean and Vile Condition," Zinn continues to lay out the history for the intentional disaffection of oppressed peoples one from another. The financial benefits to the moneyed interests from the contrived enmity between groups has worked to their advantage for generations and continues to roil our politics and our nation today. As long as we continue to blame the brown and keep "otherizing" the latest group of immigrants (we hear repeatedly that "we are a nation of immigrants"), we will remain fractured, balkanized, and largely powerless to focus our corrective attention on the real problems that face us all.

One-fifth of the population in the New World was comprised of peoples stolen from Africa and consigned to a life of uncompensated labor and mistreatment.

Through all that growth, the upper class was getting most of the benefits and monopolized political power. A historian who studied Boston tax lists in 1687 and 1771 found that in 1687 there were, out of a population of six thousand, one thousand who owned property. The top 5 percent—1 percent of the population—consisted of fifty rich individuals who held 25 percent of the wealth. By 1770, the top 1 percent of property owners owned 44 percent of the wealth.[5]

The rampant income inequality that many speak against today in the twenty-first century is not new. It has its roots from the very beginning of this nation; it's in our national DNA. The great documents that are still quoted today enunciated high ideals, but they didn't *really* apply equally to all concerned:

> **T**he rampant income inequality that many speak against today in the twenty-first century is not new. It has its roots from the very beginning of this nation; it's in our national DNA.

> to assume among the powers of the earth, the separate and equal station to which the Laws of Nature and of Nature's God entitle them … We hold these truths to be self-evident, that all men are created equal, that they are endowed by their Creator with certain unalienable Rights, that among these are Life, Liberty, and the pursuit of Happiness.

In large part, that "equal station" does not seem to apply to poor white and brown people. The "self-evident" truth that all are created equal is challenged when some leave their equality at the hospital on their way home after being born, especially if their parents are not of a particular economic or ethnic rank. The unalienable rights promise the *pursuit* of happiness. Of course, it is impossible to *guarantee* that people will achieve it, but it is much less likely if one must first overcome economic disadvantage, classism, and ethnicism to achieve it. The reality seems to be "Y'all have the right to *pursue* all you like, but if you're poor or brown, good luck with that!"

Some like to maintain that children are born a blank slate and can achieve anything they want if they will just hitch up their bootstraps and handle their business. Never mind that many children are born without access to the figurative boots or straps. *No child should be behind the eight ball from birth.* No child should be denied the opportunity to achieve, to make the choices that lead to chances to succeed. *Their station of birth should not be a permanent, systemic obstacle that prevents them from achieving and excelling.*

I have used the following illustration to help people who are not African American and/or who do not come from challenged backgrounds to understand the challenges people of color have had to face in this country.

Imagine a race where once the starting gun sounds, some folks get to take off running, while others are chained to the starting line; that's slavery. Eventually, because of the Civil War and the temporary gains of the first Reconstruction, these people get to leave the starting line and run in the race *with a refrigerator on their backs.* That's the post-Reconstruction and Jim Crow eras, the American form of apartheid (after which South African apartheid was modeled). Then, as a result of the second Reconstruction—the civil rights era, War on Poverty, Affirmative Action, and the like—African Americans were finally able to put their refrigerators down and just run. After about forty years of *somewhat* unencumbered running, trying to catch up from the aforementioned delays over a three-hundred-year period, comes all of the pushback against so-called reverse discrimination and other nonsense. This mindset essentially states, "You've had forty years to make up for three hundred years of deficits. Now you're on your own!" In what universe does that make sense? In what track meet is a person running encumbered for ten miles expected to be running even with the pack at the fourteen-mile marker? That is dishonest, it's hypocritical, and simply not realistic!

Zinn continues:

> The colonies were becoming groups of "contending classes." The country therefore was not "born free" but born slave and free, servant and master, tenant and landlord, poor and rich. The tensions and resentments by those indentured servants and new

groups of immigrants resulted in occasional outbreaks and some of those protests erupted into violence.

There was a popular uprising in France a few years ago, when the French people filled the streets in protest of their government's plans to reduce some entitlements that benefited most of the people. My wife contrasted *their* response to what usually happens in the United States by saying, "In

> The country therefore was not "born free" but born slave and free, servant and master, tenant and landlord, poor and rich.

France, the government is afraid of the people, but here in the US, the people are afraid of the government." The French people turned out in large numbers, and the government relented.

In the United States, our collective attention span is so short that the next round of games in the NFL, MLB, NBA, NHL or the next episodes of *The Real Housewives of* _____ (insert city here), *Scandal, Dancing with the Stars, Preachers of L.A., Empire, Celebrity this* and *Stars that* distract us from what is going on around us and in our *own* lives. None of these distractions has anything to do with the quality of *your* life, meeting the needs of *your* family, or elevating your life so that *your* children can live a better, more productive, and more fulfilling life than you have.

Yet, after times of momentary pique about the things that systemically weigh us, our children, and our descendants yet unborn down, our anesthetized populace returns to its homes and televisions, forgets their grievances, or simply capitulates and accepts the "fact" that things won't get any better. So why even bother? We have representatives who don't represent us and public servants who don't serve the public, but we cannot seem to mount a consistent and insistent response to their misgovernance, their benign neglect, *and* their malicious neglect. As a result, we get the government we deserve, and since People Power is largely asleep, has given up, or has been strategically balkanized and has turned against one another, we must endure the "worst government money can buy." Thus, legislation and court rulings continue to favor the top 1 percent—and the rest of us get screwed.

Returning to Professor Zinn's historical analysis on the topic of a "Mean and Vile Condition" and the manipulation and stoking of ethnic division in the formation of our nation, he addresses the challenges the wealthy faced in controlling the various population groups in this new and forming country:

> With the problem of Indian hostility, and the danger of slave revolts, the colonial elite had to consider the class anger of poor whites—servants, tenants, the city poor, the propertyless, the taxpayer, the soldier and sailor. As the colonies passed their hundredth year and went into the middle of the 1700s, as the gap between rich and poor widened, as violence and the threat of violence increased, the problem of control became more serious.

> What if these different despised groups—the Indians, the slaves, the poor whites—should combine? Even before there were so many blacks, in the seventeenth century, there was, as Abbot Smith puts it, "a lively fear that servants would join with Negroes or Indians to overcome the small number of masters."[6]

> Those with wealth and property could easily identify the areas for potential problems. The question: *"How do we control these people who collectively outnumber us?"*

> Bacon's Rebellion was instructive: to conciliate a diminishing Indian population at the expense of infuriating a coalition of white frontiersman was very risky. Better to make war on the Indian, gain the support of the white, and divert possible class conflict by turning poor whites against Indians for the security of the elite.[7] [Divide and conquer 101]

In the Carolinas, however, whites were outnumbered by black slaves and nearby Indian tribes; in the 1750s, 25,000 whites faced 40,000 black slaves, with 60,000 Creek, Cherokee, Choctaw, and Chickasaw Indians in the area. Policies were enacted that intentionally kept their enemies divided and allowed wealthy whites to maintain their tenuous control.

The white rulers of the Carolinas seemed to be conscious of the need for a policy, as one of them put it, "to make Indians and Negros a checque upon each other lest by their Vastly Superior Numbers we should be crushed by one or the other." And so laws were passed prohibiting free blacks from traveling in Indian country. Treaties with Indian tribes contained clauses requiring the return of fugitive slaves. Governor Lyttletown of South Carolina wrote in 1738: "It has always been the policy of this government to create an aversion in them [Indians] to Negroes."[8]

This states it as plainly as it can be said! There was a deliberate government policy to create an aversion in those who would soon be the victims of genocide and driven from their ancestral lands toward those stolen from their native lands. Yet in spite of all that, Zinn adds:

> There was a deliberate government policy to create an aversion in those who would soon be the victims of genocide and driven from their ancestral lands toward those stolen from their native lands.

Blacks ran away to Indian villages, and the Creeks and the Cherokees harbored runaway slaves by the hundreds. Many of these were amalgamated into the Indian tribes, married [and], produced children. But the combination of harsh slave codes and bribes to the Indians to help put down black rebels kept things under control.

It was the potential combination of poor whites and blacks that caused the most fear among wealthy white planters. If there had been the natural racial repugnance that some theorists have assumed, control would've been much easier. But sexual attraction was powerful across racial lines. In 1743, a grand jury in Charleston, South Carolina, denounced "The Too-Common Practice of Criminal Conversation with Negro and Other Slave Wenches in this Province." Mixed offspring continued to be produced by white-black sex relations throughout the colonial period, in spite of laws prohibiting interracial marriage in Virginia, Massachusetts, Maryland, Delaware, Pennsylvania, the Carolinas, [and] Georgia. By declaring the children illegitimate, they would keep them inside the black families, so that the white population would remain "pure" and in control.

[Or they could have simply asked "Massa" to sleep in his *own* house in his *own* bed with his *own* wife and to leave the "slave wenches" alone—Just sayin'.]

What made Bacon's Rebellion especially fearsome for the rulers of Virginia was that black slaves and white servants joined forces ... All through those early years, black and white slaves and servants ran away together, as shown by the laws passed to stop this and the records of the courts.[9]

People of a similar condition and station had enough sense of self-preservation to join forces for their mutual benefit.

This fear may help explain why Parliament, in 1717, made transportation to the New World a legal punishment for crime. After that, tens of thousands of convicts could be sent to Virginia, Maryland, and other colonies. It also makes understandable why the Virginia Assembly, after Bacon's Rebellion, gave amnesty to white servants who had rebelled, but not to blacks. Negroes were forbidden to carry any arms, while whites finishing their servitude would get muskets, along with corn and cash. The distinctions of status between white and black servants became more and more clear.[10]

The poor whites were *still* poor but were treated *slightly* better than the brown servants and the enslaved. Wealthy whites in Great Britain, in order to support wealthy whites in the Colonies, changed their laws to allow the forced export of whites with a criminal history, simply to augment their numbers in the New World.

Racism was becoming more and more practical. Edmund Morgan, on the basis of his careful study of slavery in Virginia, sees racism not as "natural" to black-white difference, but something coming out of class scorn, a realistic device for control. 'Your free man, with disappointed hopes, should make common cause with slaves of desperate hope, the results might be worse than anything Bacon had done. The answer to the problem, obviously if unspoken and only gradually recognized, was racism, to separate

The practical manipulation to hinder relationships between poor whites and stolen Africans planted the seeds for centuries of ethnic and economic animus—and this still works to the advantage of the wealthy to this day!

dangerous free whites from dangerous black slaves
by a *screen of racial contempt.*

The practical manipulation to hinder relationships between
poor whites and stolen Africans planted the seeds for centuries of
ethnic and economic animus—and this still works to the advantage
of the wealthy to this day!

Zinn continued:

> There was still another control which became
> handy as the colonies grew, and which had crucial
> consequences for the continued rule of the elite
> throughout American history. Along with the
> very rich and the very poor, there developed a
> white middle-class of small planters, independent
> farmers, city artisans, who, *given small rewards for
> joining forces with merchants and planters, would be a
> solid buffer against black slaves, frontier Indians, and very
> poor whites.*[11]

Now, not only was the white middle class being viewed as a
buffer between the ruling elite and stolen Africans and "frontier
Indians," it was also a buffer against very poor whites, from
whom many of the middle class had only recently escaped. Rather
than seeking to elevate everyone, people were instead essentially
designated and locked into their original status, except for the few
buffer folks who were allowed to escape. The more cities grew, the
more governments intentionally nurtured the support of skilled
white workers by making sure they didn't have to compete against
slaves or free Negroes.

This was the beginnings of labor animus between skilled white
workers and skilled brown people.

> Middle-class Americans might be invited to join a
> new elite by attacks against the corruption of the
> established rich. The New Yorker, Cadwallader
> Colden, in his *Address to the Freeholders* in 1747,

attacked the wealthy as tax dodgers unconcerned with the welfare of others (although he himself was wealthy) and spoke for the honesty and dependability of "the midling rank of mankind" in whom citizens could best trust "our liberty & Property." This was to become a critically important rhetorical device for the rule of the few, who would speak to the many of "our" liberty, "our" property, "our" country ... The term "middle class" concealed a fact long true about this country, that, as Richard Hofstradter said: "it was ... a middle-class society governed for the most part by its upper classes."

Those upper classes, to rule, needed to make concessions to the middle-class, without damage to their own wealth or power, at the expense of slaves, Indians, and poor whites. This bought loyalty. And to bind that loyalty with something more powerful even than material advantage, the ruling group found, in the 1760s and 1770s, *a wonderfully useful device.* That device was *the language of liberty and equality,* which could unite just enough whites to fight a Revolution against England, without ending either slavery or inequality.[12]

The Entrenched Abuses Continue

We continue the narrative a little over one hundred years later, marking the completion of the first century of this experiment called the United States of America. In chapter 11 of his book, entitled "Robber Barons and Rebels," Professor Zinn lays out the continuation of economic inequality, by design, and how all three branches of the government were working in sync to maintain those inequalities and to shut down, buy off, or assimilate any movements seeking to address those inequities. He also details the business acumen and exploitation of workers by J. P. Morgan, John D. Rockefeller, Andrew

Carnegie, and others, who sometimes separately, but often colluding (together), worked to control the political process while building great wealth on the backs of the poor.

> In the year 1877, the signals were given for the rest of the century: the black would be put back; the strikes of white workers would not be tolerated; the industrial and political elites of North and South would take hold of the country and organize the greatest march of economic growth in human history. They would do it with the aid of, and at the expense of, black labor, white labor, Chinese labor, European immigrant labor, female labor, *rewarding them differently by race, sex, national origin, and social class, in such a way as to create separate levels of oppression-a skillful terracing to stabilize the pyramid of wealth.*[13]

It is ironic that even today, people from humble backgrounds continue to defend, with all their might, the "right" for the wealthy to accrue even more wealth, pay as few taxes as possible, and benefit from government largesse. I don't know if they are proclaiming these things as a hedge, just in case they one day become multimillionaires or billionaires. When the wealthy have the struggling as their economic advocates, that's a pretty neat trick.

What a confounding irony how the wealthy economic classes manage to dupe poor working stiffs that they actually share the same problems, burdens, and concerns. For the wealthy, their great concern revolves around taxes and wanting to pay as little as possible. The family from the struggling economic classes is duped into believing

What a confounding irony how the wealthy economic classes manage to dupe poor working stiffs that they actually share the same problems, burdens, and concerns.

that we all are taxed too much, including those poor rich folks, who are "just like me."

A story that is always told with relish about our American can-do spirit is how after World War II, the Greatest Generation came home from war and, by sheer grit and perseverance, developed and grew into "the largest middle class the world had ever known." That didn't happen by accident. During and after World War II, the income tax rate for the highest income earners was 90 percent. That continued until the 1960s, when it dropped to 70 percent. During the Reagan administration, it was drastically cut to just under 30 percent. Today, the highest rate remains under 40 percent. So, when our troops returned home, the exceedingly high tax rate allowed for the financing of the G.I. Bill, the Marshall Plan, the interstate highway system, and all manner of enhancements to our national infrastructure and quality of life supporting our burgeoning middle class. It was no coincidence or accident.

During the 1960s, when President Lyndon Johnson was launching his ambitious War on Poverty, hoping to "end poverty as we know it," the tax rate dropped, thus providing fewer resources to help lift the nation's chronically poor out of poverty. Some gains were made, but not to the level President Johnson had hoped. By the Reagan years, the rate declined so much that, in conjunction with increased defense spending and the like, our national deficit exploded. It is difficult to cut income, raise expenses, *and* balance the budget. As a result, the national debt accrued during the Reagan years exceeded the debt accumulated by the first thirty-nine presidents combined.

I certainly am not suggesting that the highest tax rate should have remained at 90 percent. While the wealthy have unarguably been able to make the money that they have accrued in this country because of the favorable conditions of our capitalistic economy, the 90 percent rate—deemed necessary to support the nation during a time of a war and as it was concurrently emerging from the Great Depression—was unsustainable. But the many things government was able to achieve for *We the People then*, the government is no longer able to even consider now. Antitax rhetoric has become so heated and visceral that talk of *any* increase in taxes is met with intransigent opposition. Simply stated: taxes are how *We the People* (the government) pay for stuff. The lower the taxes, the less government can do. The difficulties of the past thirty-plus years were also no coincidence or accident. It's simple math: the less we take in, the less we can do, and the more some of our fellow citizens will be left behind.

> **T**he difficulties of the past thirty-plus years were also no coincidence or accident. It's simple math: the less we take in, the less we can do, and the more some of our fellow citizens will be left behind.

Zinn continues his recounting the saga of the "Robber Barons and Rebels." For them, the profit motive was primary, and everything else seemed irrelevant.

> How could dividends be paid to all those stockholders and bondholders? By making sure Congress passed tariffs keeping out foreign steel; by closing off competition and maintaining the price at $28 a ton; and by working 200,000 men twelve hours a day for wages that barely kept their families alive.

[These "Robber Barons" controlled the Congress so that they might maximize their profits while paying as little as humanly possible to their workers.]

> And so it went, in industry after industry—shrewd, efficient businessmen building empires, choking out competition, maintaining high prices, keeping wages low, using government subsidies. *These industries were the first beneficiaries of the "welfare state."*[14]

There it is: the corporate welfare so many still grouse about today. It is interesting how, whenever a disadvantaged community dares to advocate for itself, it is deemed a special interest. Yet when the business interests send in their teams of lobbyists to secure their exceptions and subsidies, it is just business as usual.

> Meanwhile, the government of the United States was behaving almost exactly as Karl Marx described a capitalist state: pretending neutrality to maintain order, but serving the interests of the rich. Not that the rich agreed among themselves; they had disputes over policies. *But the purpose of the state was to settle upper-class disputes peacefully, control lower-class rebellion, and adopt policies that would further the long-range stability of the system.* The arrangement between Democrats and Republicans to elect Rutherford Hayes in 1877 set the tone. "Whether Democrats or Republicans won, national policy would not change in any important way."[15]

The greatest casualty of this compromise was the ending of the Reconstruction period, in which much of the Negro community was essentially consigned to another century of apartheid in America.

A couple of paragraphs later, Zinn made this observation about our elections: that they "took the usual form of election campaigns, concealing the basic similarity of the parties by dwelling on personalities, gossip, trivialities." Same stuff, different day!

Even the Supreme Court played a role in maintaining the economic imbalance and limiting the full citizenship rights "regular" people. Zinn comments:

> Meanwhile, the Supreme Court, despite its look of somber, black-robed fairness, was doing its bit for the ruling elite. *How could it be independent, with its members chosen by the president and ratified by the Senate? How could it be neutral between rich and poor, when its members were often former wealthy lawyers and almost always came from the upper class?*[16]

Very soon after the 14th Amendment became law, the Supreme Court began to demolish it as a protection for Blacks, and to develop it as a protection for corporations. [As this misappropriation of the Fourteenth Amendment and other travesties sanctioned by the Court continued, by the year 1886], the Court did away with 230 state laws that had been passed to regulate corporations.

By this time the Supreme Court had accepted the argument that corporations were "persons" and their money was property protected by the due process clause of the Fourteenth Amendment. Supposedly the Amendment had been passed to protect Negro rights, but of the Fourteenth Amendment cases brought before the Supreme Court between 1890 and 1910, nineteen dealt with the Negro, 288 dealt with corporations.[17]

[Corporations as persons in the 1800s. *Same stuff, different day. The more things change, the more they remain the same!*]

Corporations as persons in the 1800s. *Same stuff, different day.* The more things change, the more they remain the same!

The justices of the Supreme Court were not simply interpreters of the Constitution. They were men of certain backgrounds, certain interests ... In 1893, Supreme Court Justice David J. Brewer, addressing the New York State Bar Association, said:

> It is the unvarying law that the wealth of the community will be in the hands of the few...The great majority of men are unwilling to endure that long self-denial and saving which makes accumulations possible...and hence it always

has been, and until human nature is remodeled always will be true, that *the wealth of the nation is in the hands of a few, while the many subsist upon the proceeds of their daily toil.*[18]

[Ah, but the proceeds of their *"wealthy* toil" were accumulated on the backs of those doing the hard work in their factories.]

A bit later, Zinn made the connection between wealth, philanthropy, and education, listing the names of some of the wealthy and their donations to start numerous universities some named in their own honor (e.g., Vanderbilt, Cornell, Duke, and Stanford).

The rich, giving part of their enormous earnings in this way, became known as philanthropists. These educational institutions did not encourage dissent; they trained the middleman in the American system-the teachers, doctors, lawyers, administrators, engineers, technicians, politicians-those who would be paid to keep the system going, to be loyal buffers against trouble.

[Educational propagandizing did not stop at the college level but was also employed at the high school level too.]

It was in the middle- and late- nineteenth century that high schools developed as aids to the industrial system, that history was widely required in the curriculum to foster patriotism.[19]

According to Zinn, another vehicle of control was the two-party system.

As the immigrants became naturalized citizens, they were brought into the American two-party system, invited to be loyal to one party or the other, their political energy thus siphoned into elections.[20]

The unstated purpose of the "two-party system" seems to be to control and undercut *any* movement in our country that might foment real, systemic change to the benefit of *We the People*. Yet we have become conditioned to rely upon these parties to allegedly act in our best interests. In essence, we have ceded control of electoral politics in our "representative democracy" to two private organizations that are maintained and funded by moneyed interests. *How's that working out for you?*

The remainder of this chapter, "Robber Barons and Rebels," examines the rise and fall of various political movements and protests in the waning years of the nineteenth century. There were agrarian movements that sought to unite black and white farmers against the landowners who oppressed them both (referenced in the quote from Dr. King in chapter 3). There were protests by workers in numerous industries, usually centered in large cities that would attempt to bring people together because of their common interests, but were always suppressed. Some, by inciting ethnic hatred between one group or the other, raised the specter of resentments by immigrants with more seniority on these shores against the more recent immigrants. Both were in the same boat—a boat filled with holes and taking on water—but the manufactured resentment between these groups of workers with similar interests was undercut by the manufactured "otherness" of more recent immigrants and African Americans.

There is a pattern in this country of assimilating and diluting vibrant grassroots movements by encouraging those whose effective movements were threatening real change to "come inside the tent." The lie is told over and over again: "You can accomplish more on the inside than you can on the outside." I remember another quote attributed to President Lyndon Johnson that I will paraphrase. He is reputed to have said, "I'd rather have you on the inside of the tent pissing out than on the outside pissing in." Translation: If you're on the inside, we pay you and therefore own you. If you're on the inside, you have to abide by our rules—the rules of the organization or the party. If you're on the inside, we can control you, dilute your movement, and funnel down your broader objectives to more narrow changes that won't upset the accepted order of things too much. On the inside, you have been co-opted. *My advice? Keep pissing from the outside!*

On other occasions, sometimes those who are already on the inside will hustle to get out in front of the march or parade that started without them, in order to assume leadership of that movement, and by extension, redirect it, slow it down, or kill it.

Clearly, there was enough fear of and concern about the Populist Movement to compel the political process (the political parties), the media, and the moneyed interests to join together to undermine it. Even after the Populists had already been somewhat assimilated into the Democratic Party (and therefore had their message diluted), the unholy trinity of party, media, and money needed to make sure that not even a viable vestige of the populist agenda would be implemented. So, in 1896, the Populist-supported Democratic Party presidential candidate, William Jennings Bryan, was defeated by William McKinley "for whom the corporations and the press mobilized in the first massive use of money in an election campaign," according to Zinn:

> It was a time, as election times have often been in the United States, to consolidate the system after years of protest and rebellion. The black was being kept under control in the south. The Indian was being driven off the western plains for good; on a cold winter day in 1890, US Army soldiers attacked Indians camped at Wounded Knee, South Dakota, and killed 300 men women and children. It was the climax to 400 years of violence [*and genocide*] that began with Columbus ... And where a threatening mass movement developed, the two-party system stood ready to send out one of its columns to surround that movement and drain it of its vitality.

Always, as a way of drowning class resentment in a flood of slogans for national unity, there was "patriotism." [Quotation marks added.] McKinley had said, in a rare rhetorical connection between money and flag:

> This year is going to be a year of patriotism and devotion to country. I'm glad to know that the people in every part of the country mean to be devoted to one flag, the glorious Stars & Stripes; that the people of this country mean to maintain the financial honor of the country as sacredly as they maintain the honor of the flag.

The supreme act of patriotism was war. Two years after McKinley became president, the United States declared war on Spain.[21]

Then vice president Theodore Roosevelt wrote to a friend in the year 1897: "In strict confidence ... I should welcome almost any war, for I think this country needs one."[22]

These sentiments, coming from a scion of one of the nation's prominent families, speaks to the use of war to rally and refocus the attention of *We the People* away from our own interests—those things that are *most* needful in our own homes and communities—to focus on some foreign "enemy" thousands of miles away. I will give Roosevelt credit; at least he was willing to go and participate in the war personally. However, the true sentiments of the moneyed interests who were controlling just about everything in the nation was more accurately reflected by the father of James Mellon.

I digress, for a moment, back to the Civil War era, when Zinn reports:

> (J. P.) Morgan had escaped military service in the Civil War by paying $300 to a substitute. So did John D. Rockefeller, Andrew Carnegie, Philip Armour, Jay Gould, and James Mellon. Mellon's father had written to him, that *"a man may be a patriot without risking his own life or sacrificing his health. There are plenty of lives less valuable."*[23]

Whiskey Tango Foxtrot! Most of the wars of this country, especially the more recent ones, have been fought to "protect our national interests." *National interests* meaning what helps to keep the moneyed interests in the money. I am assuming that helps to explain why the first casualties of our unprovoked invasion into Iraq were killed trying to secure an oilfield—and we didn't even benefit from lower oil and gas prices here at home. I guess it was simply a matter of "lives less valuable" being used to continue to secure profit for the top 1 percent. To show their gratitude, they continue to allow the families of some military members to be compelled to rely upon SNAP benefits to survive, to oppose labor agreements, pay low wages whenever possible, raise prices, and even use the largesse at their disposal—earned as a result of a favorable business climate in the United States—to move their companies overseas, a practice that costs tens of thousands of jobs in the United States. But with the okeydoke we hear and see every day, too many of my fellow citizens believe that our financial distress is entirely the fault of brown people! Really?

With those words from Theodore Roosevelt begins chapter 12 of Zinn's work, entitled "The Empire and the People." This chapter details many of the military entanglements by the United States around the world, usually to protect commerce at the expense of the loss of life for the working class and the poor.

So the language of liberty was a useful device, even employed in our founding documents, the Declaration of Independence and the Constitution. These documents encouraged hope, loyalty, and a false sense of kinship that everyone was in the same boat and that "our" *actually meant* "all of us." Yet the carefully laid and nurtured seeds of dissent between different ethnic and economic groups, even at the founding of our great nation, continues to undermine us 240 years later.

The Preamble to the Constitution reads:

> We the People of the United States, in Order to form *a more perfect Union*, establish *Justice*, insure *domestic Tranquility*, provide for the common defense, *promote the general Welfare, and secure the Blessings of Liberty to ourselves and our Posterity*, do ordain and establish this Constitution for the United States of America. [Emphasis added.]

All of the words I have italicized are those things the "better angels of our nature" desire to pursue and secure for *every* citizen of the United States. Because of the seeds of dissent, disunity, distrust, and disregard also sown at our nation's inception, we still have much work to do to truly accomplish the "more perfect union" we were promised, but that has been systematically undermined, very long ago.

I am hopeful and determined to see those platitudes come true. In order for that to happen, however, we must remember this simple axiom: "If we keep doing the same things we've always done, we will continue to get what we've always gotten." Are *We the People* sick and tired enough to make a change?

We're Number One?

In the 1960's an expression that became widely used was, "Dissent is the highest form of patriotism." As a man who loves his country and is the latest of several generations in my family to serve his country in uniform, I feel free to say this: We are *not* number one in so many of

> "**D**issent is the highest form of patriotism."

the indices that really matter. We have more nuclear weapons than the next twenty-six countries in the world combined—and twenty-three of them are our alleged allies. So in the category of defense spending, we *are* number one! But let's look at other key measures of the quality of life in this country.

In a hidden-in-plain-sight example, in the opening sequence of the HBO series premiere of *The Newsroom*, news anchor Will McAvoy, played by Jeff Daniels, is seated on a college stage between stereotypical "liberal" and "conservative" talking heads. A student asks the question, "Can you say why America is the greatest country in the world?"

McAvoy attempts to avoid responding with the brutal honesty

he would like. When pressed by the moderator, he says, "It's *not* the greatest country in the world!"

He then goes on to point out key indicators of the nation's relative health, or lack thereof.

> There's absolutely no evidence to support the statement that we're the greatest country in the world. We're seventh in literacy, twenty-seventh in math, twenty-second in science, forty-ninth in life expectancy, 178th in infant mortality, third in median household income, number four in labor force, and number four in exports. We lead the world in only three categories: number of incarcerated citizens per capita; number of adults who believe angels are real; and defense spending, where we spend more than the next twenty-six countries combined, twenty-five of whom are allies.

I wanted to fact check the data, delivered at a machine-gun pace by McAvoy. I found the following information on the rankingamerica.wordpress.com and other websites concerning how the United States ranks in key standard of living/quality of life data from 2008 to 2015:

Literacy: fifteenth (twentieth in reading at the end of 2013, according to NPR.com)

Math: twenty-fifth (thirtieth at the end of 2013, according to NPR.com)

Science: twenty-ninth (twenty-third at the end of 2013, according to NPR.com)

The comment made on the NPR.com website concerning the education numbers: "Their scores in reading, math, and science have not changed since 2003."

Life expectancy: forty-ninth (forty-third in the 2015 estimate listed in *The CIA World Factbook*)

Infant mortality: 180th (167th in the 2015 estimate listed in *The CIA World Factbook*)

Defense budget: first in the Global Firepower publication rankings of 126 nations for 2015, which was more than five times

Russia and China's spending ranked at two and three, respectively. Our defense budget was $581,000,000—that's over *half a trillion* dollars for those who are counting. Most of the remaining top twenty-five are allies, except North Korea, which ranks twenty-five. So we outspend our three "adversaries," collectively, by a factor of three to one.

We also lead the world in the number of bankruptcies due to medical expenses. (More than 60 percent of all US bankruptcies are due to medical bills.) According to a June 25, 2013, article by Dan Mangan posted on the CNBC website ("Medical Bills Are the Biggest Cause of US Bankruptcies: Study"), nearly two million people filed bankruptcy as a result of unpaid medical bills. Approximately 75 percent of those persons had health insurance! "Even outside of bankruptcy, about 56 million adults—more than 20 percent of the population between the ages of 19 and 64—will still struggle with health-care-related bills this year, according to NerdWallet Health."

I believe it was Benjamin Franklin who is credited with saying that "an ounce of prevention is worth a pound of cure." But as comedian Chris Rock noted in one of his performances, "the money isn't in the cure, it's in the comeback." While preventive care makes the most sense, *if* the health of the people is the paramount consideration, it is not the most urgent consideration if our healthcare is driven by a profit motive (aka greed). We would rather fight tooth and nail *against* Medicare for all or the public option (single-payer national healthcare), than to take meaningful preventive steps to improve the health of *all* Americans. We have the capacity to increase life expectancy (as well as enhance function in later years) rather than a bedridden illness that kills us slowly but keeps us coming back to and paying the medical-industrial complex. Because we have become so accustomed to two-dimensional, binary thinking in this country, we continue to suffer third-world-level infant-mortality rates. We feel powerless to change a system that allows corporate executives and insurance company bean counters (most of whom are not physicians and should *not* be entrusted with making healthcare decisions!) to make obscene amounts of money off of us, while not even delivering a better healthcare product. Who does this benefit?

It sure as heck ain't most of us, irrespective of ideology, skin tone, or party.

One other category where we *are* number one: we also lead the world in the number of citizens on probation or parole with six million.

Therefore, while his presentation was not entirely accurate, it was largely in the ballpark based on the data from 2011 to 2012 that they would most likely have used. I quote these statistics from one of the most well-written and intelligent programs I have seen in years because the writers worked diligently to be as accurate as possible in presenting factual information, even as they were crafting a compelling storyline. We, as a country, love to say "we're number one," but *saying* it isn't enough! Out of the list that McAvoy gives to show where we have room to improve, I find these to be the most compelling and interrelated statistics: We are first in defense spending, yet we are only forty-third in life expectancy, one hundred sixty-seventh in infant mortality, and first in bankruptcies caused by medical expenses and the number of incarcerated citizens per capita. It begs the question: How many missiles are enough? How many tanks and guns and ships and warplanes are enough? When can we begin to divert some money from defense spending to provide health insurance for every citizen? I understand that these comments run counter to our doggedly held Doctrine of American Exceptionalism, but the numbers are what they are, and the truth is what it is! The numbers don't lie; they don't tell the whole story, but they don't lie.

For the sake of example (and with apology to Cincinnati Bengals fans), that would be like the Cincinnati Bengals having a Doctrine of Bengals Exceptionalism. In spite of the fact that they have *never* won a Super Bowl and haven't *been* to a Super Bowl since the 1980s, they doggedly insist that they *are* exceptional and will browbeat into submission those who would dare to point to the actual evidence contrary to their claim. Would that make any sense? Of course not!

US Navy Commodore Stephen Decatur offered this toast at a banquet in his honor: "Our country! In her intercourse with foreign nations, may she always be in the right; but our country, right or wrong." Staying with that theme, in her interactions with her *own* citizens, may she always be right; but our country right or wrong. But *if* she is wrong, we must point out the error of her ways and do everything in our power to help her change course from a self-destructive direction. Whatever undermines any portion of our country ultimately undermines the whole.

In an interview in 2002, Professor Howard Zinn said, "While some people think that dissent is unpatriotic, I would argue that **dissent is the highest form of patriotism.**" That means if we truly love our country we will hold her accountable to be the very best she can be. We will not simply accept bromides about exceptionalism or patriotism. We will instead seek to hold our country to its highest principles and ideals—in a quest to become "that more perfect union"—even when insisting on such accountability and consistency with our stated principles is unpopular.

Chapter 6

MORE OKEYDOKE

Two wings, same bird
— Native American proverb

T he title of this book, *Stop Falling for the Okeydoke*, was chosen intentionally. Again, *okeydoke* is defined as something that is absurd or ridiculous. It can also reflect an intention or desire to swindle or to deceive. I would argue that we have been treated to the absurd and ridiculous for far too long. Our decisions about how we regard and treat other human beings based solely on the color (or lack thereof) of their skin have far-reaching consequences. At this stage of the game—and make no mistake, for those controlling the levers of power and controlling the persons who hold positions of influence (in electoral politics and the media), it *is* a game—*we* are the suckers getting played. (Thus, the cover of the book!) This game has staggering and unwelcome consequences for most people on the planet.

The driving force behind much of what ails us is *greed*; at the end of the day, this is all about the Benjamins! "Whoever loves money never has enough; whoever loves wealth is never satisfied" (Ecclesiastes 5:10). It's about the financial gain of the few at the expense of the many, and much of it is fueled by *the deliberately cultivated animus between people of different ethnicities for the sole purpose of keeping those persons—from similar circumstances, who have similar interests and concerns in life—separated from one another, based almost*

91

entirely on the skin that they're in. Irrespective of our vast similarities, will we continue to doggedly hold on to our minor differences and treat them as if they are far more significant or meaningful than they truly are? As long as our nation allows itself to continue to be divided by skin color, regardless of our collective needs or interests or what is in the best interests of the country, the political process will continue to fail us.

> **A**s long as our nation allows itself to continue to be divided by skin color, regardless of our collective needs or interests or what is in the best interests of the country, the political process will continue to fail us.

Let's be done with the Okeydoke 101, the myth where we actually believe that there are good guys and bad guys (depending upon your political or ideological points of view). If we were to approach this from a *CSI* perspective, we would look for the DNA evidence on the weapons being used to injure us (and our republic). I submit that the fingerprints of *both* the good guys and the bad guys would be found on the weapon! I paraphrase a truism from earlier in the book in chapter 5, that no matter who is in office or which party *gives the appearance* of controlling the levers of political power, "the rich will get richer, the poor will get poorer, and the middle will get screwed"— and then the poor and immigrants will get the blame for it!

Part of the balkanization is due to the misperception that the political parties in this country actually matter, as far as benefitting *We the People* is concerned. There is an old Native American proverb, "Two wings, same bird." Let me make it plain: When the Republicans are in office, the rich get richer, the poor get poorer, and the middle class gets screwed. Ah, but when

> **"T**he only difference between the Democrats and the Republicans is that the Democrats usually kiss you *first!"*

the Democrats are in office, the rich still get richer, the poor still get poorer, and the middle class still gets screwed. My father used to put it this way: "The only difference between the Democrats and the Republicans is that the Democrats usually kiss you *first!*" We have been indoctrinated to think that political parties matter with respect to our quality of life. For the most part, they do not.

Further, the political parties are *not* a constitutionally enshrined element of our government. They are not even government entities. They are private, nongovernmental organizations that establish their own rules, control the political process to such an extent as to minimize and marginalize almost any other form of political expression or dissent, and then rig the game (see gerrymandering) until the office holders choose their voters rather than the voters choosing their (alleged) representatives.

In the movie *Star Trek: Wrath of Khan*, the *Enterprise* is playing a game of interstellar cat and mouse with another ship led by Captain Kirk's archenemy, Khan. Khan was genetically engineered to be superior in every way, physically and intellectually. At a point when Kirk is trying to find something that will give him an advantage over Khan, Mr. Spock makes a simple but poignant observation: "He's intelligent, but not experienced. His pattern indicates two-dimensional thinking." Armed with that revelation, Kirk has the *Enterprise* change its trajectory from the usual backward/forward and right/left movements to also changing its movements up and down. With this subtle change, they achieve the victory.

Every aspect of political and public policy discussion in this country is approached from a binary, two-dimensional perspective that is either/or, red/blue, left/right, conservative/liberal. The game of winning out over one's *alleged* opponent (more on that shortly) supersedes actually taking the time to discern what option would provide the greatest good for the greatest

> **E**very aspect of political and public policy discussion in this country is approached from a binary, two-dimensional perspective

93

number. This two-dimensional thinking prevents us from having an open mind to ever hear from anyone not claiming to be a Democrat or a Republican. We have drunk the Kool-Aid so completely that we will not even take the time to listen to hear *if* another candidate has anything to say that makes sense to us. And although there are several candidates for president every four years, the Commission on Presidential Debates won't even consider allowing anyone who is not a Republican or Democrat to take the stage (unless they are a billionaire businessman like H. Ross Perot or a former congressman like John Anderson), to the detriment of our public discourse and the diminution of our choices. Yet every quadrennium, we allow ourselves to meander through another national election season with the same limited binary choices we had four, eight, twelve, sixteen years ago!

In a letter to Jonathan Jackson in 1780, John Adams, one of the founders of our nation and our second president, shared his concerns about a political system limited to two parties: "There is nothing which I dread so much as a division of the republic into two great parties, each arranged under its leader, and concerting measures in opposition to each other. This, in my humble apprehension, is to be dreaded as the greatest political evil under our Constitution."

One of the chief architects of our republic and the second president of the United States dreads division "into two great parties" that function in opposition to each other. I would submit that his concern was warranted and has been proven correct! At this point, these parties seem to function more as albatrosses for the nation than as assets.

Yet another founder of our country, George Washington, shared his concerns in his farewell address in 1796. As he was preparing to leave the presidency after serving two terms as our first president, he said:

> In contemplating the causes which may disturb our Union, it occurs as matter of serious concern that any ground should have been furnished for characterizing parties by geographical discriminations, Northern and Southern, Atlantic and Western; whence

designing men may endeavor to excite a belief that there is a real difference of local interests and views. One of the expedients of party to acquire influence within particular districts is to misrepresent the opinions and aims of other districts.

[See? Lying about the opposition and misrepresenting their opinions and goals is nothing new.]

You cannot shield yourselves too much against the jealousies and heartburnings which spring from these misrepresentations; they tend to render alien to each other those who ought to be bound together by fraternal affection ... The alternate domination of one faction over another, sharpened by the spirit of revenge, natural to party dissension, which in different ages and countries has perpetrated the most horrid enormities, is itself a frightful despotism. But this leads at length to a more formal and permanent despotism.

Party factionalism leads those who *should* share a common cause to become alien to one another. We ought to be bound by our common interests and "fraternal affection," but instead, the parties "alternate domination ... sharpened by a spirit of revenge." Those in the majority abuse those in the minority in the same manner in which they felt abused when they were in the minority. That is the definition of a vicious cycle if there ever was one!

President Washington's conclusion is that it becomes "horrid" and a "frightful despotism" that ultimately leads to a "formal and permanent despotism." It has, indeed, become regular, routine, systemic, permanent, and almost entirely and intentionally nonfunctional.

The Native American axiom "Two wings, same bird" brings an illustration to mind. Think about an airplane. It has two wings, and it requires both to fly. If one wing falls off, the whole plane will crash. Thus, the regular prognostications after each election cycle that the losing party is near death and extinction are overblown and inaccurate. The parties always manage to resurrect in time for the next election cycle—because the bird *requires* two wings to fly. But here's the thing: *most of us ain't even on the doggone plane!* The passenger compartment of the plane is filled with the paying customers, the chambers of commerce, Wall Street, and other representatives of the 1 percent. Occasionally, there is a guest or two on the plane. Some of the senior elected leadership gets to fly from time to time. A few might even make it into the cockpit. *Their task, however, isn't to determine the course; it is simply to fly the plane wherever the paying customers wish to go.* The entertainer or athlete who is the flavor of the month might receive a guest pass, but they are not regular passengers. The talking heads and prognosticators of radio and television receive a guest ride every now and then to make them feel important and entitled enough to continue to blather on and bloviate from whichever of the two dimensions they are expected to advocate. The rest of us? Well, some of us are the ground crew, the baggage handlers, ticket agents, airport food workers, taxi and shuttle bus drivers, and any others lucky enough to serve the paying passengers. The rest of us don't even get to come to the airport, but everything about our lives is determined by the folks on the plane who are flying over us—but they don't understand or live our lives. They probably don't even care beyond election-season platitudes and votes. Even those votes cast are limited by the accuracy of the voting machines, the manipulations of the political process, the superdelegates, and the Electoral College—the players whose votes actually script who wins. *Two wings, same bird!*

I have two brief comments on the Electoral College. In a country that holds itself to be the exemplar of the principle of one person, one vote, how can a presidential candidate receive 35 percent, 40 percent, 45 percent, or even 49.9 percent of the vote in a state and receive no electoral votes? Essentially, if your candidate didn't win your state, your voice and vote don't count. They should at least *pretend* the votes of the people matter and allocate the electoral votes proportionally to the actual votes of the voters.

Constitutional architect (and slave owner) James Madison himself stated these words about the creation of an electoral college:

There was one difficulty of a serious nature however attending an immediate choice by the people. The right of suffrage was much more divisive in the north rather than the southern states; and the latter could have no influence in the election on the score of Negroes. The substitution of electors obviated this difficulty and seemed on the whole to be liable to the fewest objections.

In a nutshell, we got stuck with the electoral college in the latter portion of the 1700s as a compromise as a result of America's "birth defect" of slavery. I hardly think we still need to be saddled by that slavery-era institution in the twenty-first century.

We must stop living the lie.

We must stop feeding the beast.

We must stop falling for the okeydoke!

Government "of the People, by the People, and for the People"?

There are some definitions of types of political power and government systems that are instructive here. We have been led to believe that the United States is a representative democracy, yet the following forms of government seem and feel a lot more accurate than this democracy we are supposed to enjoy.

> **Oligarchy:** a small group of people having control of a country, organization or institution. *A form of government in which most of the political power effectively rests with a small segment of society, typically the people who have the most wealth,* military strength, ruthlessness, or political influence.

> **Plutocracy:** a form of oligarchy; defines a society ruled or controlled by the small minority of the wealthiest citizens. Government by the wealthy; rule by the rich.

In his March 22, 2015, *Salon* article entitled "5 Signs America Is Devolving into a Plutocracy," Tom Engelhardt wrote:

> Let me make my case, however minimally, based on five areas in which at least the faint outlines of that new system seem to be emerging:
>
> Political campaigns and elections;
>
> The privatization of Washington through the marriage of the corporation and the state;
>
> The de-legitimization of our traditional system of governance;
>
> The empowerment of the national security state as an untouchable fourth branch of government;
>
> and
>
> The demobilization of "We the People."

He further lays out his thesis by speaking to:

> "1 percent elections" [the ability of billionaires to try to buy elections in the wake of the *Citizens United* 2010 Supreme Court ruling];
>
> - the "Privatization of the State" [corporations benefitting more and more when the government "outsources" its functions to corporations];
> - the "De-legitimization of Congress and the Presidency" [the perennial do-nothing Congress *does* attempt to do *one thing* with consistency: to undermine confidence in and the effectiveness of the presidency];
> - the "Rise of the National Security State as the Fourth Branch of Government" [stoking paranoia and fear in the people about *everything* such that they willingly go along

with legislated incursions on their rights and freedoms in exchange for the mirage of being kept safe]; and

- the "Demobilization of the American People" [In the face of the purchase of government by the wealthy, the utter unreliability of the three branches of government to govern in the best interests of the people they allege to serve, and the co-opting of the corporate media, many Americans are opting out of the political process and choosing *not* to participate because they no longer see the point. It's no wonder that no matter who is running for office or what is at stake, at least 40 percent of eligible voters choose to sit out our presidential elections every four years, and according to the United States Elections Project, for "off-year" (nonpresidential) elections about 60 percent of eligible voters don't participate!—By the way, there is no such thing as an "off-year election"; they *all* matter!]

Sadly, I suppose voters have concluded that there is little advantage to be gained in beating their heads against the wall in a rigged game. That is a national disgrace, and I would argue, we are getting the government we deserve and the worst government money can buy. Even in spite of the obvious systemic imperfections, the one thing "average voters" can do on par with the wealthy is vote! "One person, one vote." If enough people actually bother to *learn about the issues* and *vote for what is in the best interest of the greatest number of our fellow citizens*, and then *hold their elected "representatives" accountable, it won't matter how many billions of dollars the wealthy pour into the race; they still only have one vote each—and there's a whole lot more of us than there are of them.* Just sayin'!

The Fourth Estate is a willing partner in this misfeasance and malfeasance. We don't need news reported with ideological intent. Just give us the facts, and let us sort out the meaning for ourselves. Stop with the labels. Stop "otherizing" one another. Stop taking special care to list the party of the person being interviewed. Let us hear the policy idea, free from the tainting of an R or D, and we will figure out what is best for us and our families—without your spin. Stop treating serious candidates and political circus acts with the same equivalency. Policy prescriptions that are, at best, unserious distractions and, at worst, dangerous, should be addressed and categorized as such!

We have always been taught that we are a democracy. A democracy is defined as government by the people, especially rule of the majority. [Someone needs to tell the US Senate a majority is 50% plus one!] A government in which the supreme power is vested in the people and exercised by them directly or indirectly through a system of representation usually involving periodically held free elections. So the United States is really (in theory, if not in practice) a representative democracy. How else can we explain or justify that while over 120 million people cast their votes for president, 538 largely unknown, *unelected* electors—members of the Electoral College—determine who the president will be?

The other definition of what a democracy is supposed to be is also telling: "the absence of hereditary or arbitrary class distinctions or privileges." The steady repetition of the *same* handful of names and families for the highest office in the land and the dominance of the top 1 percent comes to mind here.

Let us further add to the mix of things undermining our country and undermining what *We the People* are supposed to be about.

- **Gerrymandering:** the apportioning of voters by their elected "representatives" through the process of drawing self-serving lines for political districts. In a January 13, 2016 *Washington Post* article, "This Is Actually What America Would Look Like Without Gerrymandering," two maps are presented in the article: the current, tortured configuration of the nation's congressional districts and a map presenting how contiguous, nongerrymandered districts would look. I contend that if more members of Congress had to run in competitive districts, they would have to be more concerned about caring for the needs of *all* of their constituents rather than serving up enough "red meat" to win primary races knowing there would not be a competitive race in the general election. That would put the electorate back in the driver's seat. Then the new marching orders for members of Congress would be, "Legislate in the best interests of your constituents and the nation—or you're fired!" Perpetual inaction and gridlock in the name of ideological purity would no longer be a viable option for any members of Congress who wanted to keep their jobs.

- **Voter-Reduction Policies.** As opposed to a true democracy (where everyone is *encouraged* to vote), our country has increasingly become a nation where voting has been made more difficult for certain groups of Americans (mostly young voters, older voters without transportation, poor voters, and brown voters) through voter ID "ballot security" laws that do not prevent the already nonexistent problem of voter identification fraud. Any system that *intentionally* perpetuates long, slow lines at the polls, plays hide-a-poll by moving polling places around without adequate notice to voters, purges eligible voters from the voting rolls, routinely has "problems with voting machines" at the *same* (minority) precincts *every* election cycle, and seeks to limit early voting and other processes that make it *easier* to vote is an undemocratic system. We should want *more* people to vote and participate in the electoral process, not fewer! It seems that politicians do not want to answer to an energized and informed electorate. Are they afraid of being held accountable?

At the beginning of the twentieth century, my great-grandfather, former North Carolina state senator George Allen Mebane prepared and compiled a short book for the National Afro-American Council entitled *The Negro Problem as Seen and Discussed by Southern White Men in Conference at Montgomery, Alabama*. Between May 8 and 10, 1900, white men from throughout the South gathered in Montgomery, to discuss "the Negro problem." Listening to the dialogue and being keenly aware of the issues, as a former Reconstruction Era legislator in the South, Mebane wrote:

> The persistent efforts to eliminate the Negro from participation in the government, as voiced by the

> Montgomery Conference, have ever been the great
> hindrances to the speedy and proper adjustment of
> all questions pertaining to the so-called problem …
> But the contest against Negro suffrage, once thought
> to have been settled for all time, is on, and is being
> waged with unceasing and increasing acrimony
> and bitterness. And thus the country (and not the
> South), is again confronted with the question: Shall
> the Negro be recognized as a man and a citizen, or
> be again forced into vassalage? (p. 5)

[It seemed that the passage of the Thirteenth, Fourteenth, and especially the Fifteenth Amendments after the Civil War would guarantee the rights of all citizens to unimpeded access to voting, but those rights were constantly being abridged and hindered, sometimes to the point of death. It would take another sixty-five years before the Voting Rights Act of 1965 *reguaranteed* the voting rights, supposedly secured at great cost of blood and our dearest treasure a century beforehand. But here we are again, in 2016, after the Supreme Court gutted enforcement for voting protections in 2010, having to wage the same fight again. It feels like Groundhog Day.]

Mebane wrote: "There is nothing between the citizen and slavery but the ballot-box, and the ballot is his proudest legacy, strongest weapon, only shield" (p. 6). "Any people who refuse freedom and civil liberty or the right of franchise to others, shall not long maintain them for themselves" (p. 8).

[How ironic that in 1900, a mere thirty-five years after the Civil War and the ending of official slavery in the United States, part of the pushback against the rights of *all* citizens was an attempt to limit the voting rights of *some* of our citizens. Now here we are, in the second decade of the twenty-first century, and those *same* games are being played yet again!]

> It seems to me that the clanking of the chains (which)
> once fettered the intellect of the white man as well as
> the person of the Negro. (p. 8)

[As Reverend Jesse Jackson said during his presidential campaign in 1984, "You cannot hold someone in the ditch unless you linger there with them!"]

Additional things undermining our country and undermining what *We the People* are supposed to be about:

- **Unreliable and easily hackable voting machines with no accurate verifiable paper trail**. (See chapter 3.)
- **The handing over of our democracy to two private organizations, aka political parties**. Again, I reiterate, most of us were not invited *to* the party. Most of us cannot *afford* to be meaningful players *in* the parties, yet somehow these two private organizations with rules that are often neither representative nor democratic (e.g., "winner take all" states and "superdelegates") have almost complete say—with the donated permission of the plutocrats, of course—concerning the outcome of elections. Our entire political process has become a political knife fight between people who *should* aspire to be Americans first, who have chosen, instead, to be Republicans and Democrats first. Who is that helping? Their loyalty is no longer to *We the People*, but to *their* party—a "party" to which most of us were not invited. The only thing the two can seem to agree on is that neither wants to see any *other* political parties or movements gain traction or prominence that gives voters more than just the same two lesser-of-two-evils options every election cycle.

> **O**ur entire political process has become a political knife fight between people who *should* aspire to be Americans first, who have chosen, instead, to be Republicans and Democrats first.

Why have I chosen to spend so much time on "politricks"

in a book decrying the debilitating fallacy of race? I'm so glad you asked. Much of our political discourse for the past couple of centuries has devolved into how to manage and hinder the personhood, personal franchise (e.g., vote), and quality of life of brown people. Whether it is declaring, in our founding documents, that stolen Africans are to be counted as three-fifths of a human being—or by bilking the original occupants of this nation, Native Americans, out of their land through a series of meaningless treaties that have resulted in their genocide, forced relocation, and warehousing on reservations, little has changed for people of color in America. This has only been made possible by making poor white voters feel that:

1) At least they're "better" than brown people.
2) Brown people are the source of all of their problems and the reason *why* they themselves are poor.
3) The votes of brown people—originally codified in the Constitution after the Civil War—were to be constantly opposed and suppressed (often through violence).
4) The votes of brown people would be considered the province and expectation of one political party. This was the case first with the Republicans, who counted on formerly enslaved people to support the "Party of Lincoln, the Great Emancipator." By the mid-twentieth century, these expectations were held by the Democrats, as a result of Franklin Roosevelt's New Deal, Lyndon Johnson's War on Poverty, and the passing of the Voting Rights Act of 1965, which solidified the brown vote as the virtual property of the Democratic party, even as former Dixiecrats and white Southerners became Republicans.

There is also an arrogance—almost a *contempt*—for the American people that *each* party presents. I find many liberals/progressives to be very smug, self-assured, and paternalistic. They think they are smarter than everyone else, and anyone who doesn't get them or disagrees with them is just stupid. The disdain with which they hold a significant portion of their fellow citizens is not lost on those citizens either, and so conservatives have pretty much made up their minds that hell will freeze over before they accept or agree with policies advanced by liberals/progressives, because they feel dismissively and equally disrespected. It doesn't even matter if some of those policies might be in those citizens' best interests. How can these liberals/progressives ever expect to win over roughly half of our balkanized electorate if they look down on them as unintelligent rabble?

Not to be outdone, the arrogance of conservatives is that if anyone disagrees with them, it's because they just didn't clearly understand their positions. Since we obviously didn't understand how their policies were better for us (even if they have demonstrably failed in the past; see "trickle-down economics"), they must protect us from ourselves by forcing their will on us anyway. The conservatives are fond of saying that "elections have consequences," but *only* those that turn out the way they want! So, in our current political morass, were the results of the elections of 2008 and 2012 (when around 60 percent of eligible voters participated) mistakes made by an electorate who didn't know what was best for them? Did the elections of 2010 and 2014 (when 41.8 and 36.7 percent of eligible voters participated, respectively) represent the true will of the people? Really? Thus, this cognitive dissonance allows a party that claims it loves all things Constitution to govern (or *not* govern) in a way adversely opposed to the Constitution. In 2016, did the Republicans actually refuse to fulfill their constitutional duties to even *meet with*, interview, and vote upon the president's nominee to the Supreme Court—because the elections of 2008 and 2012 didn't somehow count? They choose to ignore the wishes of over 130 million people who entrusted the presidency and judicial appointments to the victor. They decided to wait the president out to see if the next election would produce results of which *they* approve. Any American who cares about things being done, as we say in the church, "decently and in order," should be troubled by this!

Even in the midst of this current nonsense, note that the balance has been maintained—poor whites and disaffected southerners on one side, and brown people and young people on the other. But as fictional senator Jay Billington Bulworth said, "Rich people have *always* stayed on top, by dividing white people from colored people. But white people got more in common with colored people than they do with rich people." In the visceral and almost pathological obsession with keeping brown people down, many of the states of the former Confederacy in the Deep South occupy the lower echelons of almost every statistical measure in this country, whether it be healthcare and life expectancy, quality of public schools, and poverty, rather than serving all of their citizens equally.

"You cannot hold someone in the ditch unless you linger there with them!"

Chapter 7

NOW WHAT?

When you know better, you have to do better!

For some of you, the information shared in the previous pages is nothing more than a review of what you already know and have been saying for years. For many others, the presentation of new information will hopefully warrant some kind of constructive, comprehensive response. I return to the premise I stated near the beginning of this book: "When you know better, you have to do better!" The precision of scientific discovery by the Human Genome Project and others informs us that at our core—our fundamental, genetic essence—*we are more than 99 percent the same.* We are less than one-tenth of 1 percent different. No matter what you learned at the kitchen table or grew up hearing from your parents, grandparents, and great-grandparents, we are all much more alike than we are different, and *that knowledge, that information,* warrants a useful response.

Learning to See

Because of the way we have been conditioned since the earliest days of the colonies and our republic, we have become accustomed to accept as normal animosity between brown people and white people. Earlier, in chapter 2, I referenced the old Native American proverb about walking in the moccasins of another; it is often difficult to impossible to truly walk in the shoes of another. How can we pretend to be someone else? How can we even accurately imagine what it's like to be someone we are not? How can we possible experience things about which we have no real clue? We can't. Instead, *what we truly need to do is learn to use another lens when seeing the world.*

It has been said that much of our disconnect from one another is caused by "inattentional blindness." Inattentional blindness, also known as *perceptual blindness,* is "a psychological lack of attention that is not associated with any vision defects or deficits." It may be further defined as "the event in which an individual fails to recognize an *unexpected* stimulus that is in plain sight. It is the failure to notice a fully visible but unexpected object because attention was engaged on another task, event, or object."

It reminds me of the scene from the 1995 movie *The Tuskegee Airmen,* where the white bomber pilot came to the base where the 332nd Fighter Group (the Tuskegee Airmen) was based. The pilot said he wanted to thank the pilots who protected his bombers, thus allowing them to finish their mission and make it safely back to their base of operations. When informed that the Negro pilots he could see all around were those pilots, he said, "This isn't right. Let's get out of here." The young captain continued to argue with the lieutenant who accompanied him. "This isn't right. I don't give a s—— what he said. Them pilots was niggers, and niggers weren't flying them planes today."

Later that evening, after the lieutenant had confirmed through headquarters and shared with the captain that the black pilots of the 332nd were indeed the ones who had protected them, he says, "Lieutenant, let me give you a little sociology lesson. I think being from California and all, you might be a little bit confused. Now I'm a Texas boy. I grew up with niggers. I was around them every day. Hell, in Lubbock, you can't throw a rock without hitting one. Now I know how they think, and I know how they live, and I can tell you with complete certainty what they are and are not capable of."

The lieutenant, clearly miffed, asks, "And you don't think they could fly *them* planes, sir?"

The captain responds, "If they was flying them planes—and that's one hell of a big if—then it was a fluke, so forget about it."

In spite of the all-Negro crew of pilots and maintenance staff being the *only* folks he could see, and the unmistakable and distinctive red tails on the planes on the tarmac, he was unable to allow himself to recognize and accept that the skilled fliers in the air earlier that day were the Negroes he was seeing right then. He had a "perceptual blindness," something not associated with any actual vision defect or deficit, that caused him to fail to recognize the unexpected stimulus plainly in his sight: *brown* pilots! He was so locked in on the cultural norms he had come to accept as true, that in that moment, he could not broaden his mind to accept a new and very apparent truth. The world, *his* world, was still flat!

As Ralph Waldo Emerson put it, "People only see what they are prepared to see."

Psychiatrist and philosopher Frantz Fanon refers to this kind of disconnect from reality as cognitive dissonance:

> **P**eople only see what they are prepared to see.

> Sometimes people hold a core belief that is very strong. When they are presented with evidence that works against that belief, the new evidence *cannot* be accepted. It would create a feeling that is extremely uncomfortable called cognitive dissonance. And because it is so important to protect that core belief, they will rationalize, ignore, and even deny anything that doesn't fit in with the core belief.

> There are two ways to be fooled. One is to believe what isn't true; the other is to refuse to believe what is true.
>
> —Soren Kierkegaard

> You are entitled to your own opinion, but you are not
> entitled to your own facts.
> —Senator Daniel Patrick Moynihan

It's Time to Get Healed

At its 2016 National Convention, NAACP chairperson Roslyn Brock stated that racism is "an insidious disease." We the People need to work for and insist upon a nation that is free of bigotry, discrimination, ethnicism, classism, and hatred. *"We don't all have to have the same mind to mind the same things!"* (From the film *Our American Vote* that was aired at the 2015 NAACP convention.)

Poet Maya Angelou said, *"History, despite its wrenching pain, cannot be unlived, but if faced with courage, need not be lived again."* Once enough of us get sick and tired of *being* sick and tired, tired of letting the lie of race hinder our lives and our nation, we can then have the courage to face the changes we need to make. These changes will be both internal (within each individual who is ready to stop falling for the okeydoke) and external (systemic changes in our society and in our government).

The miseducation of the nation (and the planet) essentially tells one group of people that they are fundamentally and inherently better than other groups of people. As the British would say, "Bollocks!" The sooner we all disabuse ourselves of any false and unprovable notion of "superiority," the sooner we can come together as people with common interests and hold those who have been holding us *all* back accountable! We must stop living the lie, stop encouraging the lie, stop giving a safe place and succor for lies to be told and believed, whether it is in our local barbershop or beauty salon, in school, in church, at the temple, at the mosque, at the family dinner table, or while offering commentary on television. Just stop it!

This cancer of ethnicism is so pervasive that it led a white father (with a swastika tattoo on his arm) to insist that no African American nurses attend to his baby in the neonatal ICU (NICU) at the Hurley Medical Center in Flint, Michigan, in 2012. The hospital foolishly yielded to this man's prejudice and posted a sign on the assignment clipboard outside the baby's room stating "No African American nurses to take care of baby." Really?

Interestingly, the first nurse the father wanted banned from the room had twenty-five years of experience and was probably the most experienced nurse in the NICU. What kind of vile seeds have been sown in this country over the years that a parent would choose to have less-experienced people care for a sick child and possibly risk an unfavorable outcome? Is our ethnicism really so pathologically entrenched that some of us are willing to let our children die, rather than receive the best possible care available from a black nurse? An old saying comes to mind here: "The Lord looks out for children and fools" [and the children *of* fools?]. Fortunately, with the experienced nurse directing things from behind the scenes, the child survived. That's just plain scary, ignorant, and unthinkable. For their role in supporting this foolishness, the hospital paid out at least $200,000 to several nurses affected by this restriction. I bet it won't do that again!

Tolerance vs. Inclusion

A huge disservice perpetrated upon people who *think* they want to become more open and welcoming to people of other ethnicities is the use of the word *tolerance*. School districts and universities say they want their students to practice tolerance. Employers counsel their employees to be tolerant. Politicians pat themselves on the back for being tolerant. Let's look at the word and see what it *really* means. Tolerance has been defined as "the ability or willingness to tolerate something, in particular the existence of opinions or behavior one does not necessarily agree with."

Tolerance is the act or capacity of enduring; suffering something. When we use the word *tolerance*, we are going through the *act* (acts, in this context, are often inauthentic) of enduring or suffering something. I am going to "endure" your distinctiveness and your differences from me. I'm going to "suffer" or "tolerate" your ethnicity and your culture. Well, isn't that big of me?

Tolerance is a willingness to accept feelings, habits, or beliefs that are different from your own. When it comes to feelings, habits, and beliefs, it does involve a willingness to accept; because one must *make the decision* to be willing to engage others—your fellow human beings—on a human level. One must decide to meet them where they are and accept that they feel how they feel, that they are who they are, and they believe the things they believe. As long as those feelings, habits, and beliefs do not disrespect or cause violence to someone else, "you do you." But when we say that we are *willing* to accept *how* a person is, in essence, we are saying, "I *accept* how the Lord made you. I accept how brown or light your skin tone is. I accept the physical features that you have." That sounds good, right?

Who are you to "accept" anything about me? That implies that who I am and have been created to be requires *any* act by or from you at all; your acceptance is neither desired nor required. I do not need your acceptance or tolerance concerning the way I am made; that it is an intrinsic, ontological fact. *It is what it is,* just as *I am who I am.* No amount of plastic surgeries (should *I choose* to subject myself to them) can ever change who I really am. I can get cut and redesigned all I want, but my children will *still* bear the imprint of my original design.

Tolerance is also defined as "the ability to accept, experience, or survive something harmful or unpleasant." Again, I assert that even beginning with the premise that your distinctiveness is something harmful or unpleasant that I have to "survive" is insulting. I understand that is not what people *intend* when they use the term *tolerance,* but it is an unspoken aspect of tolerance that people often subconsciously convey.

Tolerance is "the act of allowing something." I am *allowing* you to be who you are? Really?

The word *tolerance* is also used with respect to machinery, but even part of *that* definition is illuminating and instructive. In this context, it is "the allowable deviation from a standard; especially the range of variation permitted." Think about that in the context of another human being. My tolerance of you reflects the "allowable deviation from the standard." Don't get it twisted; *my* family and *my* own ethnic presentation and group *are* that standard! There is a "range of variation" that is permitted, and then after that, you've gone too far. You're out of bounds. You have exceeded the boundaries of uniqueness or variation or difference that I am willing to suffer or allow—to *tolerate*. Friends, that is insufferably arrogant! Again, I understand that is not what people *intend* to communicate when they speak of tolerance, but these are some of the unspoken aspects, whether we wish to claim them or not.

Instead, I would suggest that *inclusion* is a more appropriate word than tolerance to use with respect to ethnic diversity. Tolerance is the attitude of the "higher" toward the "lower": "We will tolerate you. We will suffer your existence, your differences, and your uniqueness." Instead, inclusion goes beyond any assessment or judgment phase of others and moves right to my receiving you as you are, simply *because* you are. Period! Inclusion means we "include, comprehend, comprise, and embrace." We don't keep you "over there" or create a special section where it is safe for you to express your uniqueness and distinctiveness; we *welcome* you to be with us and to be a part of us. We comprehend that there are things that make you unique, and we accept those things unconditionally (how can someone conditionally accept aspects of you that you cannot change?) We will comprise and embrace who you are into who we are, because you are and have always been a part of we, anyway! As the Borg would say in *Star Trek*, "Your distinctiveness will be added to our collective."

Let us revisit the definition of okeydoke one more time: "okeydoke" is defined as something that is absurd and ridiculous or something that is designed to swindle or deceive. Over the course of the existence of our republic, we have been treated to the absurd and the ridiculous, as highlighted in the excerpts from Professor Zinn's work, most notably in chapters 2 ("Drawing the Color Line"), 3 ("Persons of Mean and Vile Condition"), and 11 ("Robber Barons and Rebels").

So, by engaging in the okeydoke of divide-and-conquer politics and using whatever absurd and ridiculous appeals and rationales that resonated, the top 1 percent have been able to swindle and deceive most of the people in our nation for more than two centuries. Rather than pursuing and yielding to "the better angels of our nature," we have become short-sighted, isolated, and divided. Instead of focusing our fire where it belongs—on those who profit from the divisive seeds that have been sown—we continue to aim at the wrong targets. We blame brown people for everything that is going wrong in our society. As President Lyndon B. Johnson said, "If you can convince the lowest white man he's better than the best colored man, he won't know you're picking his pocket. Hell, give him someone to look down on and he'll empty his pockets for you."

If a 1 percenter decides to move his manufacturing enterprise outside of the United States to avoid regulations and taxes and to pay lower salaries, how is that the fault of "aliens"? (A term that suggests they're from another planet, right?) We spend as much time blaming Latinos who came to our country fleeing oppression in their native lands or seeking opportunities for a better life here as we did blaming the English, Irish, Italians, Germans, Eastern Europeans, and every other group of immigrants before them.

I submit that, rather than focusing on the less than one-tenth of 1 percent of our DNA that diversifies us, often to the exclusion of *everything else*, we need to pay attention to what really matters. *Follow the money. Who's getting paid? It is certainly not most of us!*

We must stop focusing on party labels, owned by organizations that did not even invite us to the party or save us a seat on the plane. Agree to agree where we can and work together where we can. Commit to honest debate with others—and vote when we cannot. Make a decision! *No one should be diametrically opposed to someone else 100 percent of the time.* Choose to be a part of the solution, rather than the problem. We have been fighting the wrong battles and losing the war (or, more accurately, We the People have been used as pawns in their war). Instead, we need to focus on our common humanity, our concerns, and our shared objectives—those things that unite us and do not divide us. We must ask ourselves and answer the following questions:

> *No one should be diametrically opposed to someone else 100 percent of the time.*

- What do I need for my family to survive and thrive?
- How can the public schools in *our* country better serve my children and *all* children? This is not a competition between communities or between school districts. "A rising tide lifts all boats" comes to mind here (assuming, of course, that *all* the boats are seaworthy).
- How can we advance career training and opportunities for our citizens to have a living wage with which they can support their families in the twenty-first century?
- How can we take our country back—from corporations, Wall Street, and political elites who are more concerned about *their* bottom line or their own party's brand than they are about the nation they allege to serve? Remember this: while We the People may not have the financial largesse to control things, everything those with financial largesse are able to accomplish is done on our backs. As Dr. King said, "A man can't ride your back unless it's bent." We must stand up and advocate and fight for what is in *our* best interests!

It's past time to *stop falling for the okeydoke*! Take the time to find allies with whom you share a common condition and common economic and political interests, regardless of the skin they're in. By doing so, we can inspire a political and economic revolution in this country unlike any seen in the history of the world where "all men [and women] are created equal, that they are endowed by their Creator with certain unalienable Rights, that among these are Life, Liberty and the pursuit of Happiness."

This is the promise of our country to which we are all heir, notwithstanding the nation's original "birth defect." However, we cannot accomplish it alone. We must do it *together*. That depends upon *you*. You have to decide to *change your mind,* to *change your attitude,* and to *change your perspective*. The world is *not* flat, and we can no longer continue to live as though it is.

It's past time to stop falling for the okeydoke!

115

POSTSCRIPT
"LIVES MATTER!"

I have been writing this book in the midst of some cataclysmic events and changes in our nation. Though addressing these particular things has never been a vision of this project, I feel compelled to share my thoughts. In the past several weeks, we have seen two men who appear to have been murdered by the police. This act has caused exceptional uproar, in part because it was captured on video. I wish that I could say this was an unusual or rare occurrence, but at the time of this writing (July 17, 2016), this is becoming a disturbing "normal" in America. According to *theguardian.com*, 598 people were killed by police in 2016 thus far—and 147 of these victims were African American; *24.5 percent of those killed by police in America in 2016 were African American.* In a country where African Americans are 13 percent of the population and African American men are approximately 6 percent of the population, that translates to almost one in four people killed by police being African American men. Ninety-four of these people, or 15.7 percent, were Latino. That, at least, is consistent with the Latino population in this country, which is 15 percent. Of the dead, eighty-eight were unarmed; of those eighty-eight, twenty-five were African American and fifteen were Latino.

Into this crush of negative statistics and tragic video images stands the Black Lives Matter movement. Launched several years ago after the murder of Trayvon Martin, the movement truly gained momentum after the shootings of Michael Brown, John Crawford III, Tamir Rice, and numerous others. Unfortunately, the binary, two-dimensional nature of public discourse in this country has created a dynamic where many people who are *not* brown are preternaturally unable and unwilling to acknowledge that there is a problem. Further, they imply that because the movement focuses on the disproportionate deaths of African Americans, it is, by extension, saying that other lives do not matter. That has never been stated or implied, but it is the rubric through which those who *preemptively* wish to discredit the issues and concerns the movement are trying to address choose to see the situation. Supporting or affirming one person or community does not, by extension, mean that we are discrediting or diminishing another community.

> The binary, two-dimensional nature of public discourse in this country has created a dynamic where many people who are *not* brown are unable and unwilling to acknowledge that there is a problem.

A law professor, in response to an anonymous complaint from a student about a Black Lives Matter (BLM) shirt worn to class, stated the following: *"There is a difference between focus and exclusion. If something matters, this does not imply that nothing else does …* Black Lives Matter is about focus, not exclusion." In the same way that a focus on Jewish lives leading up to and during World War II would warrant a Jewish Lives Matter response, BLM is appropriate and timely. In the same way that the mistreatment and deaths of thousands of Chinese working to build our transcontinental railway system in the 1800s would warrant a Chinese Lives Matter movement, BLM is appropriate and timely. Without wanting to sound harsh, *white people need to understand and accept that everything isn't about you.* There are over 7 billion people on the planet, and the majority of them are people of color. Everyone gets a turn, when circumstances require it.

Right now, circumstances also require that we affirm loudly and often that Blue Lives Matter. The targeted killing of police by some unhinged and enraged people, allegedly from the African American community, is unnecessary, unwelcome, and harmfully divisive.

No one individual life matters more than another—but none matters less either! While I understand the anger and frustration of my brothers and sisters at the almost-routine deaths of our brothers and sisters at the hands of law enforcement, that in no way justifies the murder of law-enforcement officers, most of whom simply want to do their jobs and go back home to their families.

I am privileged to serve about a half-dozen law-enforcement officers as pastor. They are human beings with the same hopes, aspirations, faults, and frailties as everyone else. Yes, they have the "authority" granted by law to take a life in exigent circumstances, but it is not—and should not be—the first option or order of business for them.

Let me be clear that *the murders of police cannot be ascribed to or blamed on the entire Black Lives Matter movement, any more than the murders of nine people in Bible study last year should be blamed on all white people or all southerners. The acts of the deranged and the hateful belong to them and them alone.* Even when they try to ascribe their motives to a particular movement (BLM in Dallas; seeking to foment a race war in South Carolina) their actions belong to them!

Right now, ISIS gladly takes credit for every unclaimed act of mayhem around the world. Does that mean they actually had anything to do with it? Not necessarily. Now, of course, the difference with ISIS is that they actually seek to recruit people to become martyrs who murder unarmed and innocent men, women, and children. If any of these people claiming this on behalf of Islam bothered to read and study the Koran first, they would see those types of killings of unarmed noncombatants is expressly *prohibited* by the Koran. The actions taken under the banner of Islam should not be ascribed to that faith group as a whole, any more than the murder of a doctor killed while serving as an usher in church on Sunday morning should be ascribed to all evangelical Christians or all pro-life advocates. The actions of evil and deranged people should not be ascribed to larger groups of people who may share some of their sentiments but do not share their methodology.

Until we reject the comfortable, familiar, unimaginative, and unproductive two-dimensional conversations we are having, we will never come to a place of mutual regard and mutual respect. We all need to be convicted enough that we will stand in opposition to the suffering of others. It matters—simply because it is happening to another member of the human family. We can either do the usual, which of late seems to be storm to our separate corners and scream at one another, or we can *listen* to one another, first to understand and then to be understood. Remember: if everyone is screaming at the same time, no one is hearing anything!

I thank Mike, an Air Force colleague and friend, for introducing me to Grammy-nominated country music artist Ronnie Dunn, who wrote a song in 2011 entitled "Bleed Red." The lyrics reflect the need for us to see one another as human beings who are all suffering, all need to be understood, and all need to both forgive and be forgiven. The main theme from the song is that we need to free ourselves to apologize to one another—before it's too late. We need to let the anger dissipate. We need to try to forgive one another (for whatever the offense might be), because we all bleed red!

In part, the lyrics caution us:

"If we're fighting, we're both losing,
We're just wasting our time
Because my scars,
They are your scars, and your world is mine.

"Sometimes we're strong; sometimes we're weak,
Sometimes we're hurt, and it cuts deep.
We live this life, breath to breath,
We're all the same, we all bleed red."

REFERENCES

Introduction

Quote in Dedication attributed to Neil Postman, *The Disappearance of Childhood*, (New York: Vintage Books, 1984)

Chapter 2

Angier, Natalie. "Do Races Differ? Not Really, Genes Show." *New York Times*, 8/22/00.

Einstein, Albert. "The Negro Question." *Pageant* magazine, January 1946.

Nye, Bill. Commencement address at Rutgers University, NJ, May 2015.

Abdul-Jabbar, Kareem. "Ignorance vs. Reason in the War on Education." *Time* magazine, 9/23/15.

King, Jr., Dr. Martin Luther. Speech at the conclusion of the Selma to Montgomery March. 3/25/65.

Chapter 3

King, Jr., Dr. Martin Luther. Speech at the conclusion of the Selma to Montgomery March. 3/25/65.

"The Food Stamp Capital of the US Is White and Republican." *Political Blindspot*, 2/3/14.

Delaney, Arthur. "Who Gets Food Stamps? White People, Mostly." The Huffington Post, 2/28/15.

Levitt, Justin. "A Comprehensive Investigation of Voter Impersonation Finds 31 Credible Incidents Out of One Billion Cast." *Washington Post*, 8/6/14.

Fitrakis, Bob. "Voting Paper Trail Advocate Dies in 'Tragic Accident.'" *Free Press*, 3/20/04.

Williamson, Kevin. "Appalachia, the Big White Ghetto." *National Review*, December 2013.

Chapter 5

1   Howard Zinn, *A People's History of the United States* (New York: HarperCollins, 2003), 28.
2   Ibid., 36.
3   Ibid., 37.
4   Ibid., 38.
5   Ibid., 49.
6   Ibid., 53.
7   Ibid., 54.
8   Ibid.
9   Ibid., 55.
10 Ibid., 56.
11 Ibid.
12 Ibid, 57–58.
13 Ibid., 253.
14 Ibid., 257.
15 Ibid., 258.
16 Ibid., 260.
17 Ibid., 260–261.
18 Ibid., 261.
19 Ibid., 263.
20 Ibid., 266.

21 Ibid., 295.
22 Ibid., 297.
23 Ibid., 255.

Chapter 6

Engelhardt, Tom. "5 Signs America Is Devolving into a Plutocracy." *Salon Magazine*, March 22, 2015.

Mebane, Geo. Allen. *"The Negro Problem": As Seen and Discussed by Southern White Men in Conference, at Montgomery, Alabama.* Prepared and Compiled for the National Afro-American Council. New York: The Alliance Publishing Company, 1900.

ABOUT THE AUTHOR

Stephen A. Tillett served twenty years in the U.S. Air Force and has been a pastor for the past twenty-seven years as well as a community activist in Maryland. He is the author of numerous columns and political commentary and is committed to the unification of the human family.

CPSIA information can be obtained
at www.ICGtesting.com
Printed in the USA
BVOW08s2114310517
485724BV00009B/16/P